Beginner Mobile App Development using MIT App Inventor 2

BY LORNA TIMBAH

Beginner Mobile App Development using MIT App Inventor 2
by Lorna Timbah

ISBN 978-967-16240-0-5

Cover and book design by Lorna Timbah (books.lornatimbah.com)
MIT App Inventor 2 logo by Massachusetts Institute of Technology

Publisher:
Lorna Timbah
PO Box 21144
Luyang Post Office
88768 Kota Kinabalu
Sabah, MALAYSIAN BORNEO

First Printing, February 2020

Preface

I started this workbook in 2018, a time where there were countless options and tools available for anyone to build any app for any platform with little to no cost. As beneficial as that may be, this poses a major challenge for those who simply want to learn and make their own mobile app: what should I use? Where do I start? Which programming language or tool should I use? The "who" I am referring to can be anyone, really. This ranges from someone with no computer programming background, a high schooler, self-taught coding hobbyist, or a person who is moving from a web platform development to native mobile app development, to parents and friends who want to be part of the current technology and just wants to "build an app".

I use different technologies and tools to develop web and mobile apps. Nevertheless, where teaching mobile app development is concerned, I always return to using visual programming tools such as App Inventor to deliver these lessons, due to two reasons.

The first reason is that App Inventor focuses on the basic building blocks of app development, separating front-end and back-end development. This allows learners to focus on creating apps that solve problems, while sparing them the struggle of understanding specific syntaxes that different programming language inherits. Indeed, learning a programming language can feel like learning a foreign language in itself.

The second reason is that using App Inventor is almost frictionless compared to other mobile app making tools like Android Studio, Eclipse, Xamarin and similar others. I personally find that the scariest part when it comes to teaching programming is in setting up the development environment; Murphy's Law is a good friend of mine during these times. Due to the web-based, ubiquitous nature of App Inventor, I can spend more time to focus on teaching development, instead of debugging software on different computer operating systems.

The limiting factor of using and teaching with App Inventor is always about getting a stable Internet connection, and it continues to be my challenge when bringing programming curriculums like this to the rural areas.

This book is mostly a compilation of many Creative Commons content prepared by AppInventor.org, MIT's App Inventor team, and various other educators and developers who have shared their content online, and which I have noted in the References. As such, all content in this book respects and is licensed under the Creative Commons, as my way of expressing my utmost appreciation for their hard work and dedication preparing the materials. This is the same content I use to teach beginners and non-programmers of all ages, and I hope this benefits you, too.

I thank the educators throughout Sabah, Malaysian Borneo, particularly Sharon Pascol and SMK Sri Nangka, Tuaran, as well as Siow May Yun and SMK Labuan in the Federal Territory of Labuan, for inviting me and supporting me in sharing the joys of programming and app development with them and the students. I dedicate this book to all educators, and to the cool dudes Eric, Ezra, and Edry, and particularly Joel for being this book's first proof-reader. You guys are the best!

Table of Content

Section 1: Introducing MIT App Inventor 2 (AI2)

What is MIT App Inventor?

App Inventor is a free open source web application based on Google's Blockly, and currently maintained by Massachusetts Institute of Technology (MIT). App Inventor allows someone who is new to computer programming to build mobile apps for Android smartphones. Many of the mobile apps look simple, yet App Inventor allows you to create more complex, data-driven apps that are limited by your creativity.

MIT App Inventor focuses on visual programming. Instead of typing out text and commands, you drag and drop graphical elements (represented by Lego-like blocks) that contain normal programming vocabularies and syntaxes into the app. Therefore, your focus will be more on learning the concepts and terms of app development and computer programming, rather than learning a specific computer programming language like Java, JavaScript, Python, or PHP.

An example of the Lego-like graphical elements in visual programming such as App Inventor

In addition, because App Inventor is browser-based, you can access the app on any operating system that has a graphical browser interface, such as Google Chrome, Mozilla Firefox, Safari, or Microsoft Edge. As long as you have a stable Internet connection, you can use App Inventor without the need for software updates. App Inventor is currently accessible at http://ai2.appinventor.mit.edu.

The user-friendly and intuitive nature of App Inventor makes it a fantastic tool to teach computer programming to anyone at any level or any age. The only requirement, apart from having access to a computer with an Internet connection, is that you have the necessary basic skills of reading, writing, arithmetic, and operating a computer. More importantly, your willingness and focus to learn mobile app development will definitely help you succeed in building your very own mobile app on Android for personal use.

Anatomy of App Inventor

Designer editor

The Designer editor, or simply `Designer`, is where you lay out the look and feel of your app, and specify what functionalities it should have. You add onto the user interface things like Buttons, Images, and Text Boxes, and functionalities like Text-to-Speech, Sensors, and GPS.

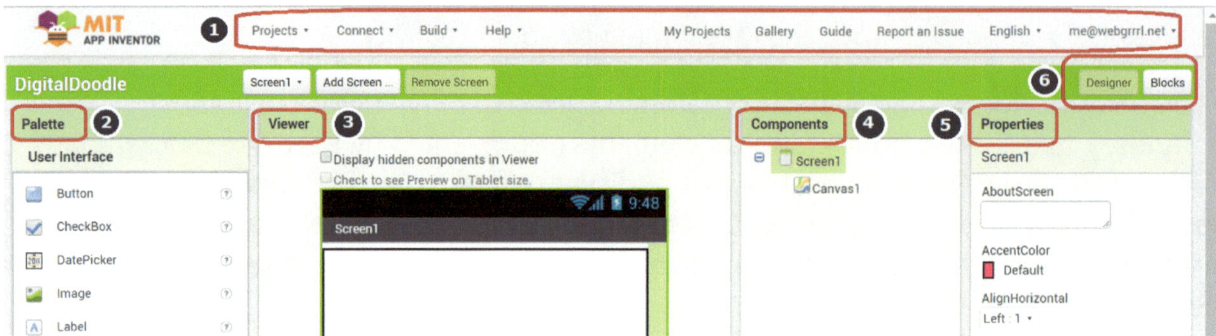

1. The **Menu bar** contains the standard system options you can use for App Inventor, including connecting your app to your phone for testing, as well as building your app into an APK package to distribute on other Android devices. Use the `Help` and `Guide` menus to access other tutorials and learn more about App Inventor.

2. The **Palette pane** contains the things you can add into your app, like user interface components and mobile phone functionalities.

3. To use the components in the Palette, you drag the component into the **Viewer pane**. You can see how your app looks like in the Viewer.

4. The **Components pane** is a list of components that you have added into the Viewer. This pane will display both visible (what you see on the screen, like buttons, text, and images) and non-visible components (what you don't see on the screen, like phone sensors). We will learn more about non-visible components in Section 3.

5. A Component has different properties and attributes associated with it, for example colour, height, alignment, and so on. When a component is selected in the Components pane, you see its attributes in the **Properties pane**, where you can then change.

6. The **Designer / Blocks switcher** are buttons that control our views between the Designer editor and the Blocks editor.

Blocks editor

The Blocks editor is where we handle events, controls and logic of our app. This is where we program each component that we added through the Designer. In programming, an **event** is an action that occurs as a result of the user or another source, such as a mouse being clicked, or a key being pressed.

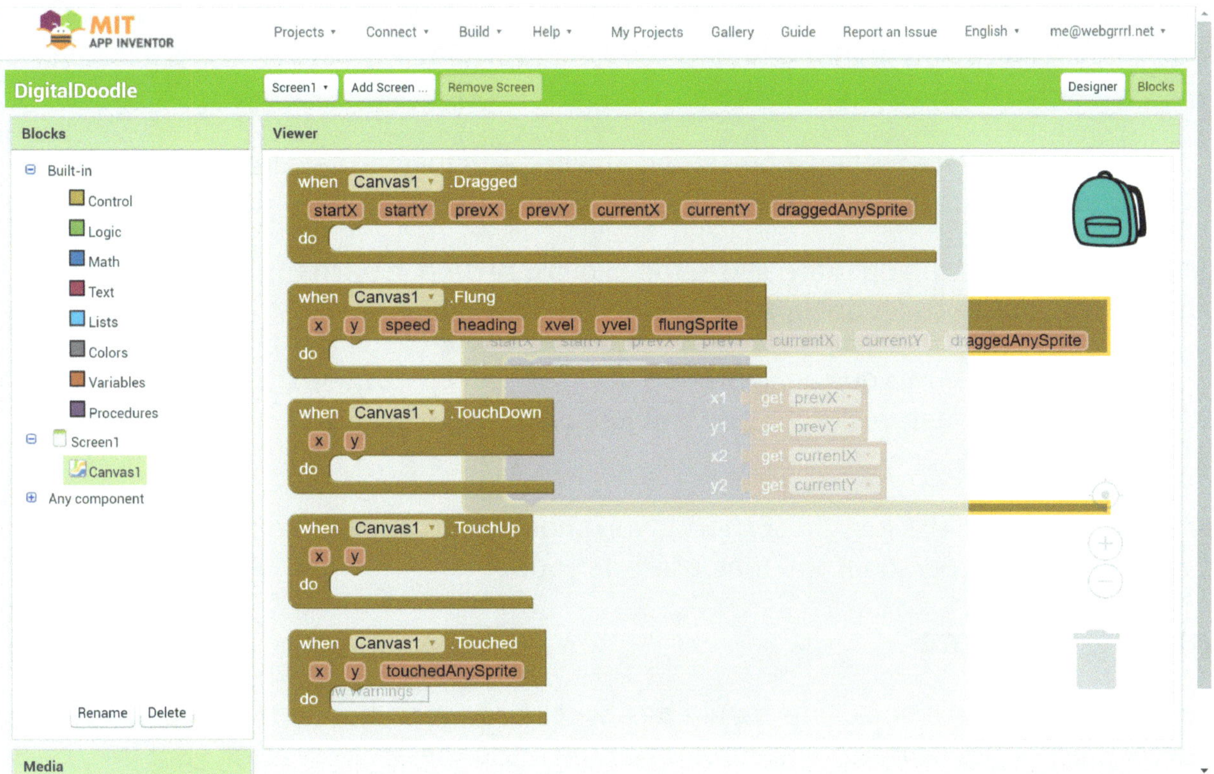

1. The **Blocks pane** contains the event handlers and components in the form of drag-and-drop blocks. An **event handler** is a routine that is used to deal with an event, allowing a programmer to write code that will be executed when the event occurs. When you click any of the blocks, a drawer opens beside it containing all related events for the component.

2. The **Viewer pane** is where you drag and drop the blocks that you selected in the Blocks pane. Here is where you snap the blocks together to set the behaviours of the app.

What We Will Learn

This book is created to allow you to complete your learning outcome of creating a simple personal mobile app for Android in less than 24 hours. You can do this individually, or as a group.

This book uses a "Build, Conceptualize, Customise, Create" learning model. Each section follows a do-first structure that has worked well in motivating learners to explore beyond what is covered in their learning sessions.

As soon as you complete Section 2 on setting up your App Inventor environment, you will start to **build** your first app in Section 3 using a step-by-step tutorial.

After you complete each app tutorial, use the Explore section in each tutorial to recap what you have done and discuss **conceptual** questions about the app.

Based on your discussion, you can figure out how you can **customise** the app by changing or adding interesting features to the app you just built. This is where Section 4 comes in handy.

After you complete all the apps in Section 3, you should finally be ready to come up with and **create** your own personal app that interests you.

Learning outcome

Upon completion of this book, you should be able to build your own mobile app for Android smartphones using App Inventor, and customise the apps to create your very own unique mobile app for personal use.

► MUST-READ: How to use this book ◄

Sections with a smiley face ● contain hands-on instructions that you are REQUIRED to do in order to achieve the learning objective of this book. Other sections of this book will help you extend your apps beyond what you have explored in the hands-on instructions.

Focus on these ● topics to QUICKLY and SATISFACTORILY complete this book.

Section 2: Setting Up Your App Inventor Environment

You can set up App Inventor and start building apps in minutes. The Designer and Blocks Editor run completely in the browser. To see your app on a device while you build it (also called "Live Testing"), you'll need to follow the steps, depending on which option you choose.

Option One (Recommended):
If you are using an Android device and you have a wireless internet connection

Build your project on your computer

Test it in real-time on your device

- You can start building apps without downloading any software to your computer. You will need to install the App Inventor Companion App on your device. This is the easiest way to test your apps.

Option Two:
If you do not have an Android device

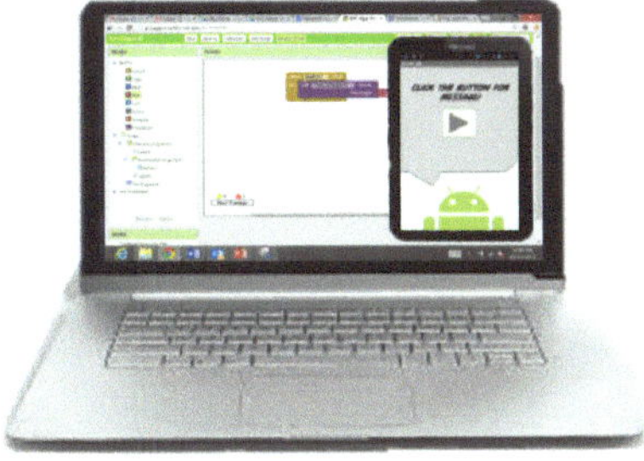

Build your project on your computer   **Test it in real-time on your computer with the onscreen emulator**

- You will need to install software on your computer so that you can use the on-screen Android emulator. If you are working in groups and don't have enough devices, you can work primarily on emulators and share a few devices with each other.

Option Three (Last Resort)
If you do not have a wireless internet connection

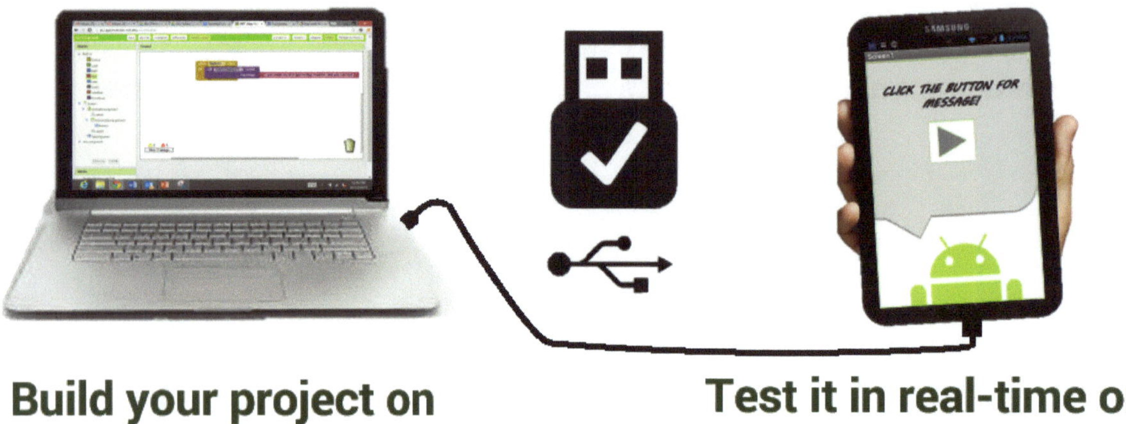

Build your project on your computer

Test it in real-time on your device

- You will need to install software on your computer so that you can connect to your Android device over USB. Some firewalls within schools and organizations do not allow the type of WiFi connection required. If WiFi doesn't work for you, try USB. The USB Connection option can be tricky, especially on Windows.

For brevity, this book will ONLY cover setting up for Option One. Option Two and Option Three will be covered briefly. Use the latter two options only if necessary.

● Option One: Connect your Phone or Tablet over WiFi

You can use App Inventor without downloading anything to your computer! You'll develop apps online at http://ai2.appinventor.mit.edu. To do live testing on your Android device, just install the **MIT App Inventor Companion app** on your Android phone or tablet. Once the Companion is installed, you can open projects in App Inventor on the web, open the companion on your device, and you can test your apps as you build them.

Step 1: Download and install the MIT AI2 Companion App on your phone

Open your device's QR code scanner and scan the QR code on the left below to download the Companion App from the Play Store. If you can't use the Play Store, use the QR code on the right to download the Companion App directly to your phone.

Google Play Store
Recommended: Automatic updates

APK File
Manual updates required

Scan this QR code or search for `MIT AI2 Companion` in Google Play Store

Scan this QR code or visit http://appinv.us/companion in your mobile phone to download directly

After downloading, step though the the instructions to install the Companion app on your device.You need to install the MIT AI2 Companion only once, and then leave it on your phone or tablet for whenever you use App Inventor.

> *Note 1: If you are unable to use the QR code, you can still install MIT AI2 Companion on your phone or tablet. Use the Web browser on your device to go to the Google Play Store; look for MIT AI2 Companion in the store. Once you find Companion, click the INSTALL button for the Companion app.*

> *Note 2: If you choose not to go through the Play store and instead load the app directly (aka "side load"), you will need to enable an option in your device's settings to allow installation of apps from "unknown sources". To find this setting on versions of Android prior to 4.0, go to "Settings > Applications" and then check the box next to "Unknown Sources". For devices running Android 4.0 or above, go to "Settings > Security" or*

"Settings > Security & Screen Lock" and then check the box next to "Unknown Sources" and confirm your choice.

Step 2: Connect both your computer and your device to the SAME WiFi Network

App Inventor will automatically show you the app you are building, but only if your computer (running App Inventor) and your Android device (running the Companion) are connected to the same WiFi network. Ideally, our network situation should look something like the image below.

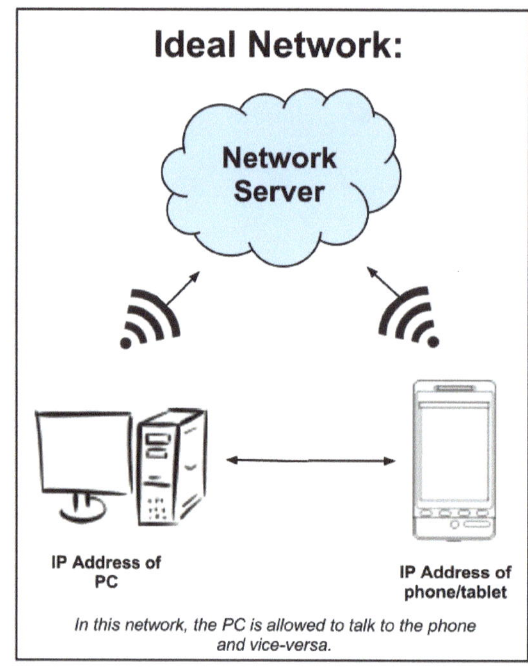

The MIT AI2 Companion app allows a user to make a connection between the Android device and your PC over the MIT RendezVous Server. The Android device must be using WiFi and NOT the cellular network for Internet connectivity.

Step 3: Open an App Inventor project and connect it to your device

Go to App Inventor and open a project (or create a new one -- use Project > Start New Project and give your project a name). Then Choose "Connect" and "AI Companion" from the top menu in the App Inventor browser.

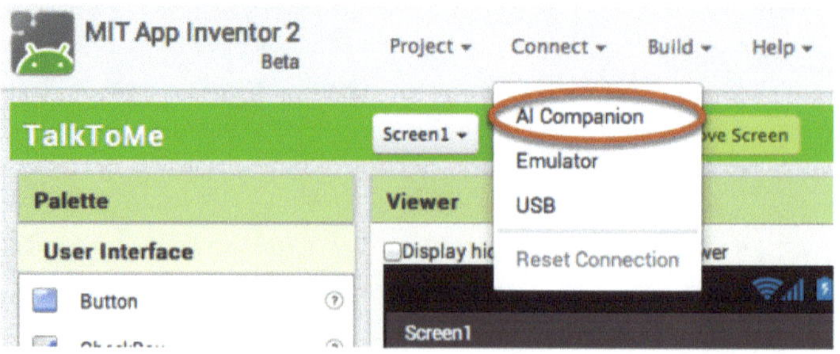

We will go over a thorough instruction for Step 3 when we start building our first app, Talk To Me, in the next section.

Option Two: Installing and Running the Emulator in AI2

If you do not have an Android phone or tablet, you can still build apps with App Inventor. App Inventor provides an Android emulator, which works just like an Android but appears on your computer screen.

The limitation to using an emulator is that some of the functionalities such as detecting motion, using near-field communication (NFC), and anything needing physical manipulation on a typical smartphone cannot be tested on an emulator.

Visit http://appinventor.mit.edu/explore/ai2/setup.html for the step-by-step guide to installing the emulator.

Option Three: Connecting to a Phone or Tablet with a USB Cable

Some environments such as hotels, conference centers, and schools, configure their wireless networks to prohibit two devices on the network from communicating with each other. When this happens, then testing your app with a USB connection is the way to go.

Setting up a USB connection can be tricky, especially on Windows machines, which need special driver software to connect to Android devices. Unfortunately, different devices may require different drivers, and, outside of a few standard models, Microsoft and Google have left it to the device manufacturers to create and supply the drivers. As a consequence, you may have to search on the Web to find the appropriate driver for your phone. If you are on a shared computer, then installing these extra drivers might be a problem.

App Inventor provides a test program that checks if your USB-connected device can communicate with the computer. You should run this test and resolve any connection issues before trying to use App Inventor with USB on that device.

Visit http://appinventor.mit.edu/explore/ai2/setup.html for the step-by-step guide to set up your computer and device using a USB connection.

Section 3: Building Your First Android App

● Project 1: Talk To Me

This step-by-step tutorial will guide you through making a talking app.

1. To get started, go to App Inventor on the web. In your browser (Google Chrome or Mozilla Firefox preferred), visit http://appinventor.mit.edu, and then click the orange "Create apps!" button from the App Inventor website.

2. Log in to App Inventor with a Gmail or Google username and password.

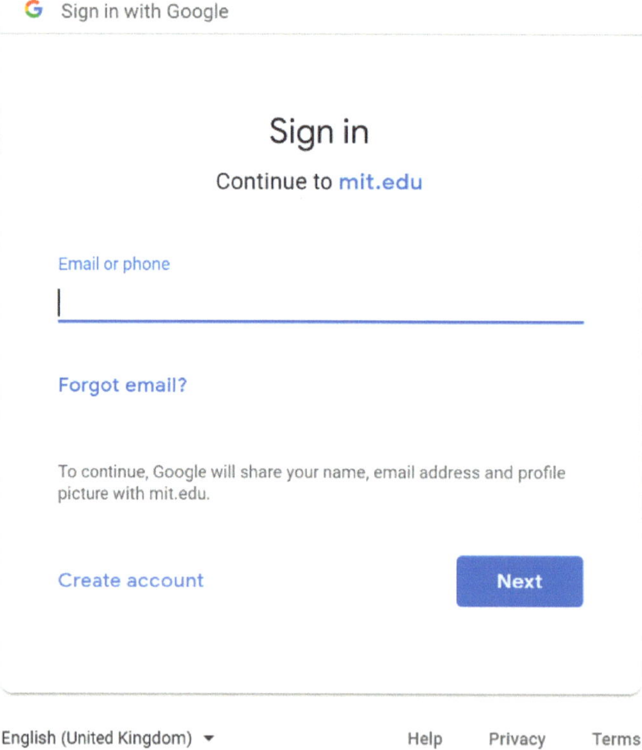

3. Click to accept the Terms of Service, and choose the appropriate buttons if you encounter any notice prompts.

4. Click on the `Start new project` button to create a new app.

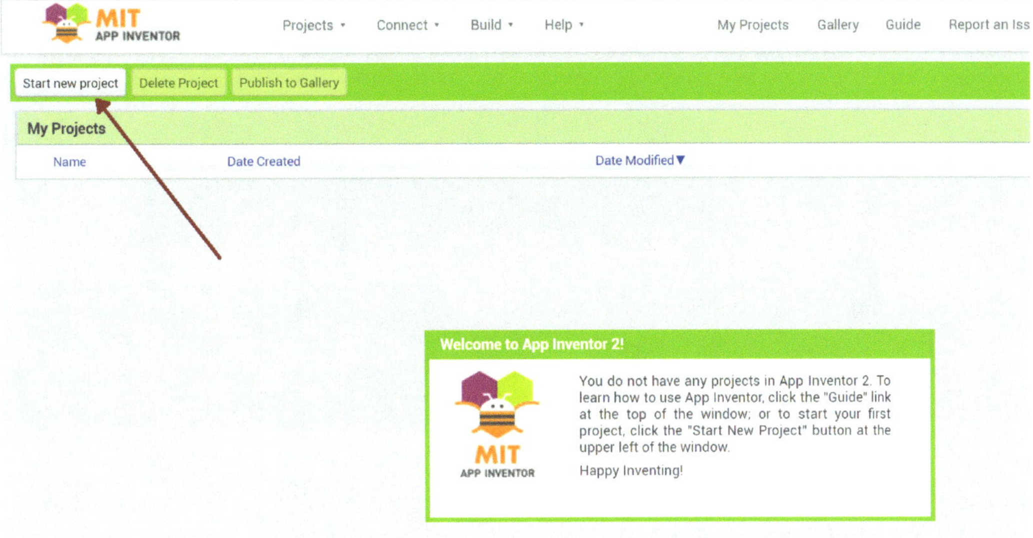

5. Type in the project name as `TalkToMe`. Spaces are NOT allowed, while underscores are acceptable. Then click OK.

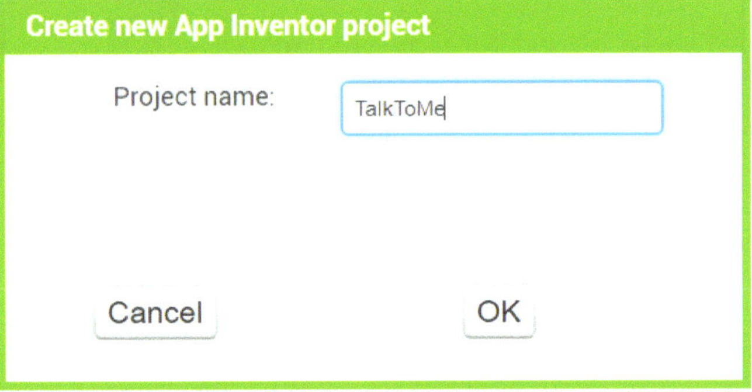

6. You are now in Designer.

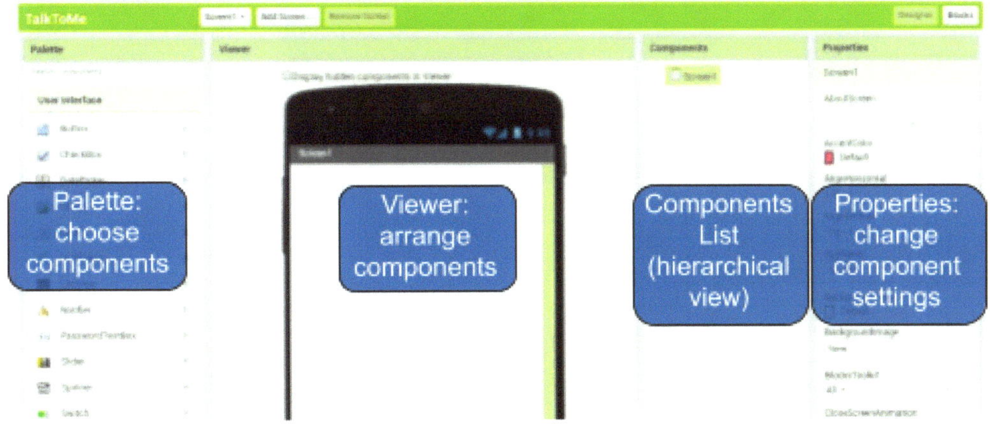

7. Add a Button component. Click and hold your mouse button on the word `Button` in the `Palette` pane. Drag your mouse over to the `Viewer` pane. Drop the button (by letting go of your mouse button) and a new button will appear on the Viewer.

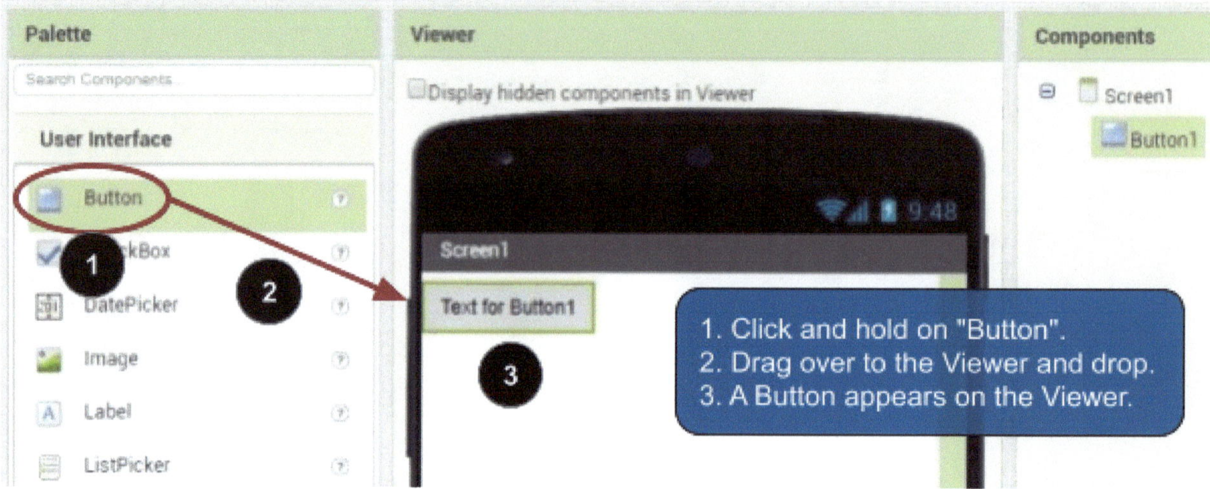

8. Start the MIT AI2 Companion app in your phone for live testing. Make sure you already installed the Companion in your mobile phone; if you haven't, follow the setup instructions in **Section 2: Setting Up Your App Inventor Environment**, then return to this tutorial.

9. On the `Connect` menu, choose `AI Companion`.

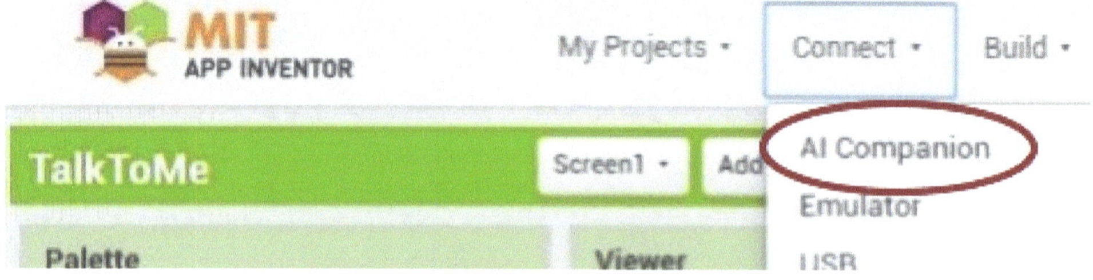

10. Scan or type the connection code from App Inventor into your Companion app.

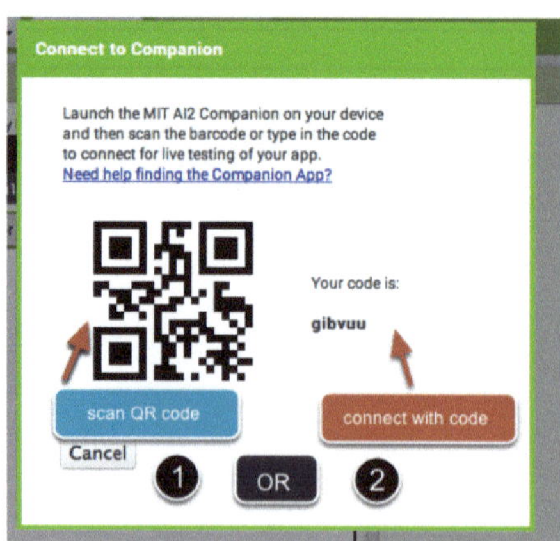

11. See your app on the connected device. So far, our app only has a button, so that is what you will see. As you add more to the project, you will see your app change on your phone simultaneously.

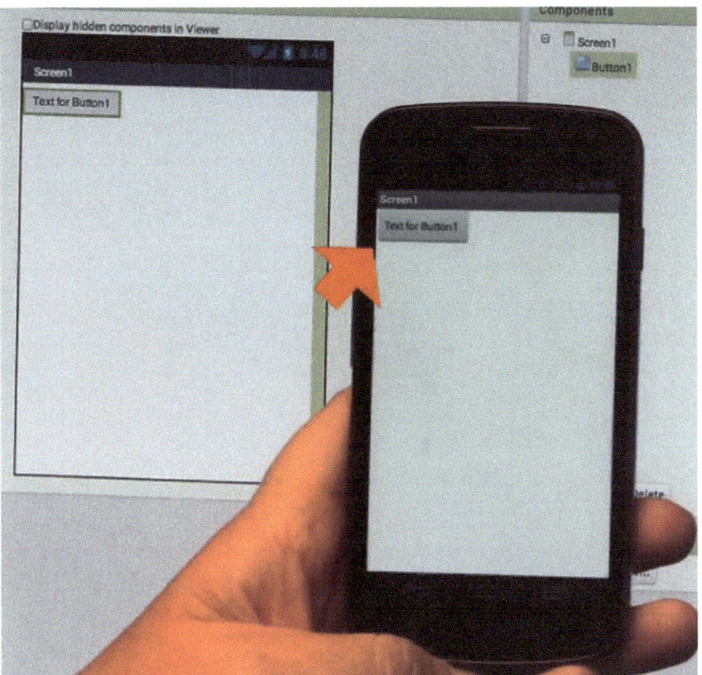

12. Change the Text on the button. On the `Properties` pane, find the `Text` property. Then, delete the default text, and type in the words `Talk To Me`. Notice that the text on your app's button changes right away.

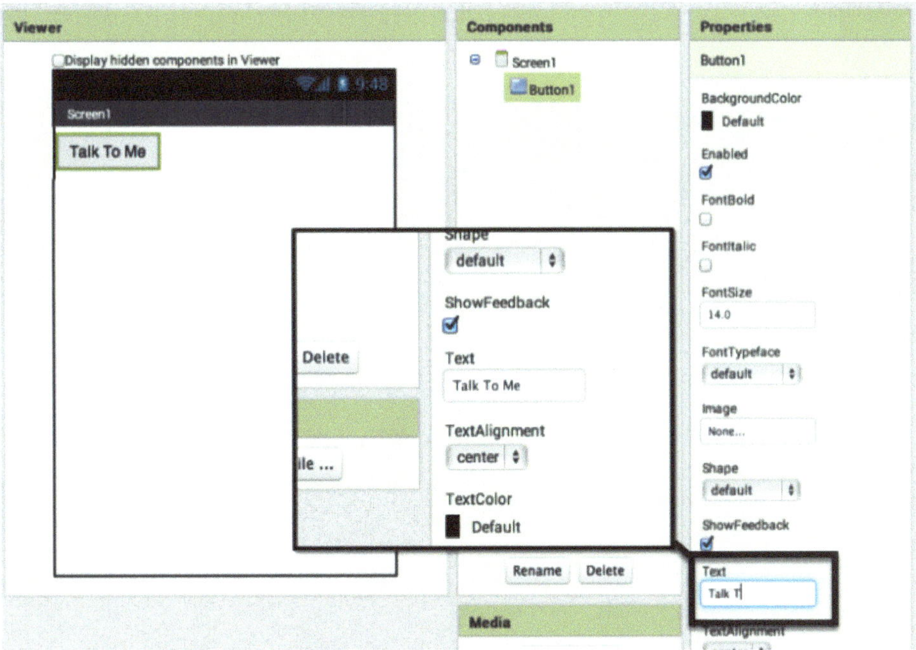

13. Add a Text-to-Speech component to your app. Go to the `Media` drawer and drag out a `TextToSpeech` component. Drop it onto the `Viewer`.

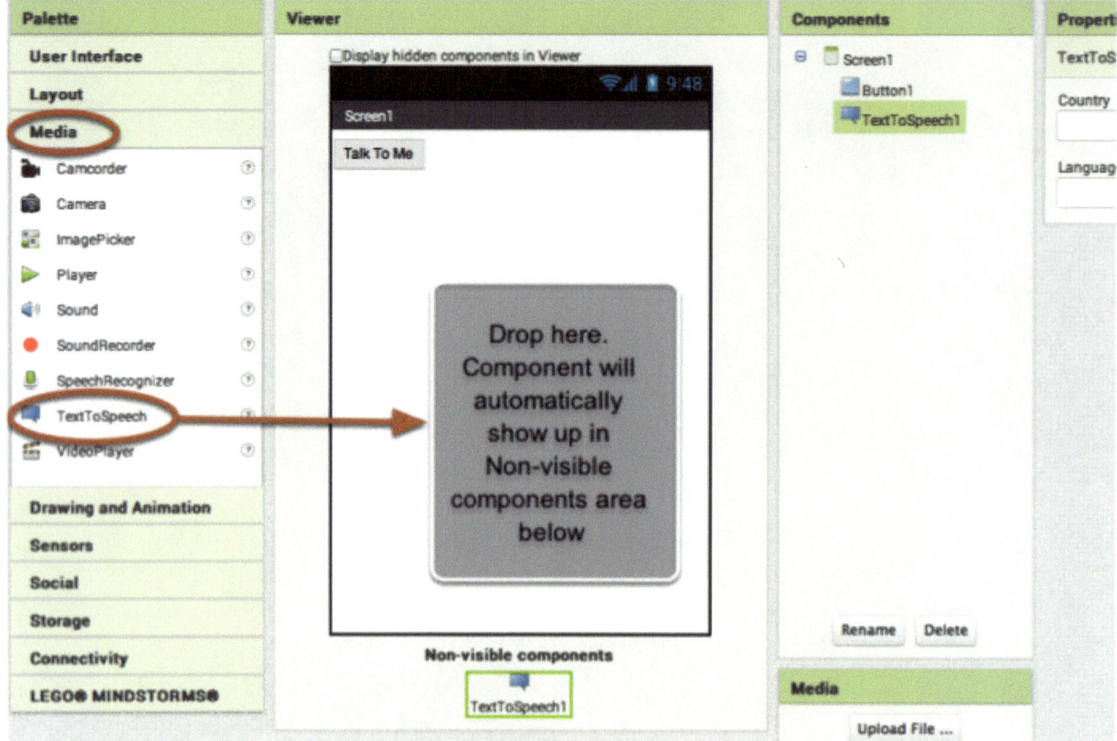

Notice that it drops down under "Non-visible components" because it is not something that will show up on the app's user interface. It's more like a tool that is available to the app.

14. Switch over to the `Blocks` editor, because now it's time to tell your app what to do!

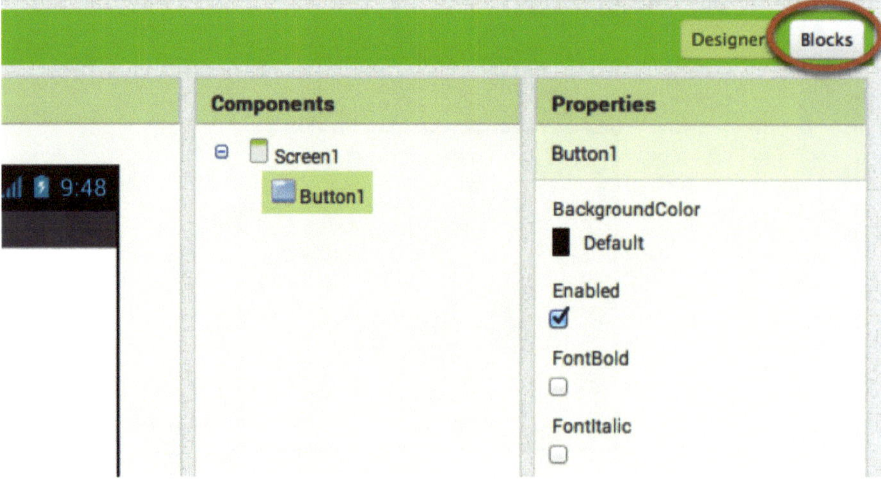

The Blocks editor is where you program the behaviour of your app. In order to get the blocks for a certain component to show up in the Blocks editor, you first have to add that component to your app in the Designer editor.

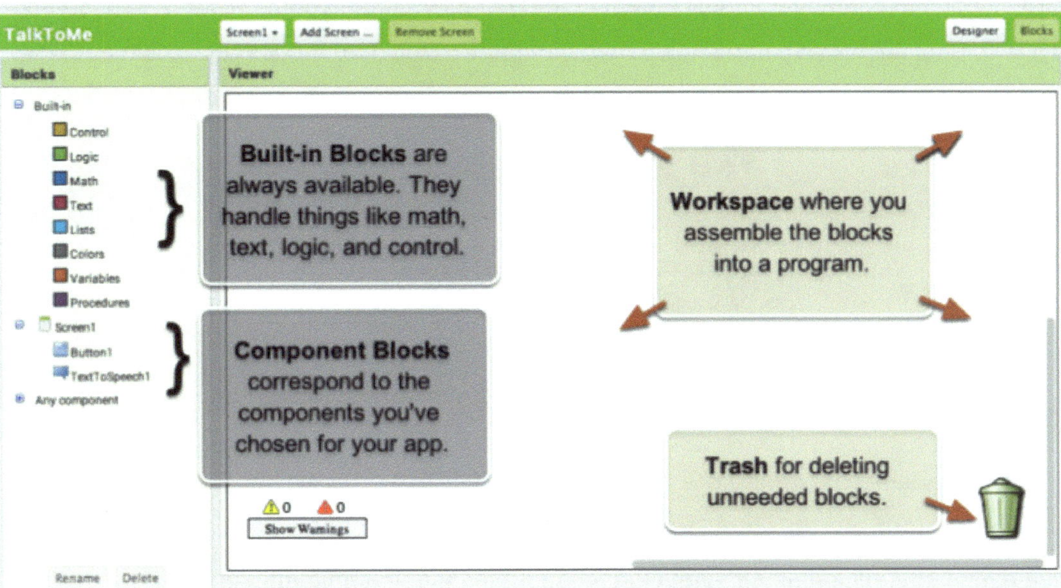

15. Make a button click event. Click on the `Button1` drawer. Click and hold the `when Button1.Click` do block. Drag it over to the Viewer workspace and drop it there. This is the block that will handle what happens when the button on your app is clicked. This is called an **Event Handler**.

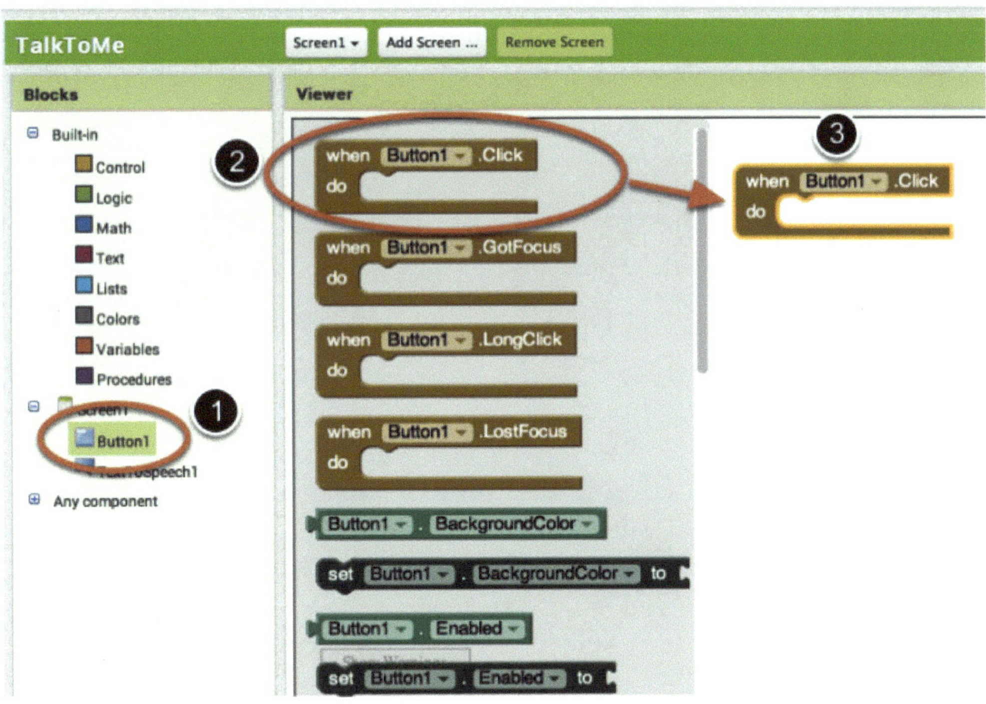

16. Click on the `TextToSpeech` drawer to program the TextToSpeech action. Click and hold the call `TextToSpeech1.Speak` block. Drag it over to the workspace and drop it into the `when Button1.Click` event handler.

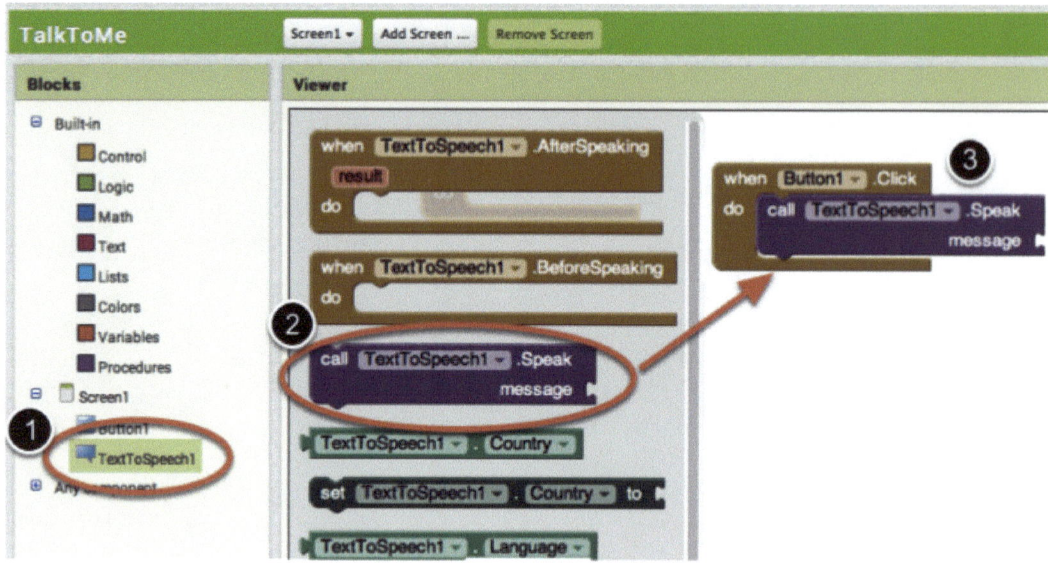

This is the block that will make the phone speak. Because it is inside the `Button.Click` event, it will run when the button on your app is clicked.

17. Now you just need to fill in the message socket on `TextToSpeech.Speak` block. To tell it what to say, click on the `Text` drawer, drag out a text block, and plug it into the socket labelled "message".

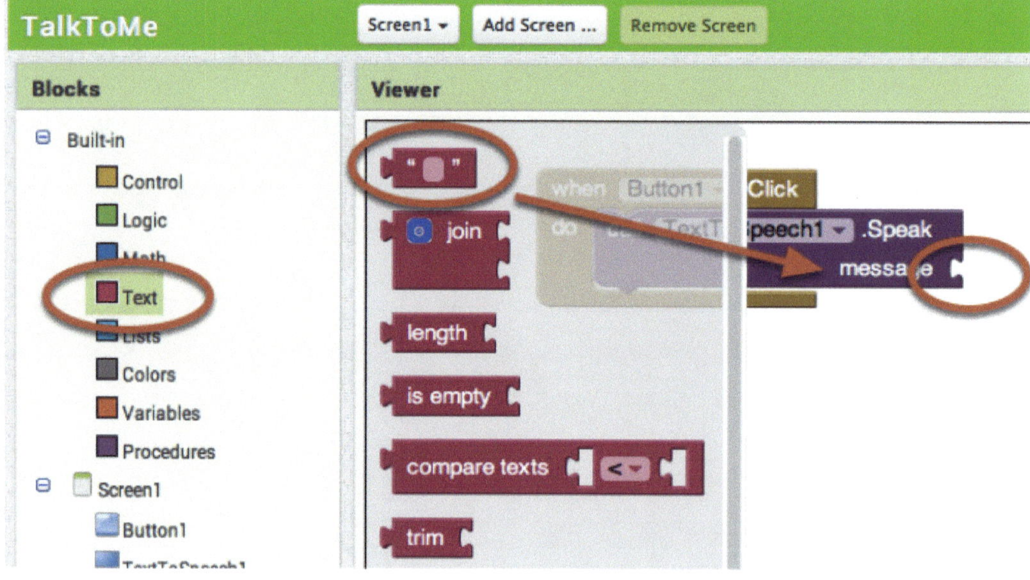

18. Click on the text block you have just plugged to specify what the app should say when the button is clicked. Type in "Congratulations! You've made your first app." (You can type in any phrase you like, this is just a suggestion.)

19. Now test it out! Go to your connected device and click the button. Make sure your volume is up. You should hear the phone speak the phrase out loud. This works even with the emulator.

Great job! Now let's extend your app to make it speak when your phone is shaken.

20. If you have closed your Talk To Me project, open the project again by clicking on it in the Projects list in App Inventor. Remember to go to http://ai2.appinventor.mit.edu to access App Inventor.

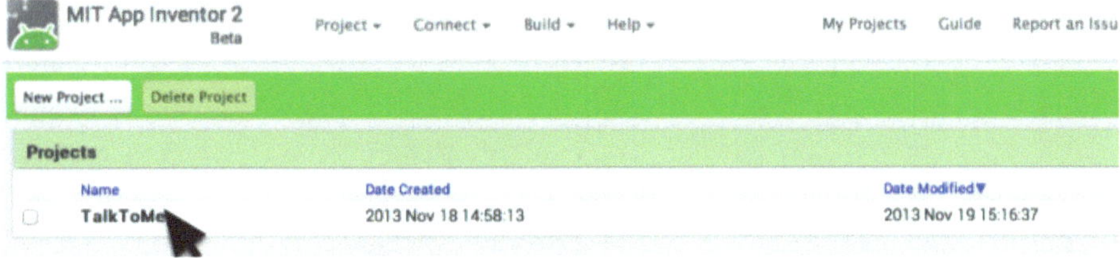

21. Go to the Designer editor by clicking on the switch on the upper right of your screen, if your project doesn't open in already.

22. ***If you are using the emulator to test your app, you should skip this part and proceed to the next instruction of this tutorial called* Say Anything!** To add an accelerometer sensor, go to the Sensors drawer, drag the AccelerometerSensor component, and drop it into the Viewer. This is a non-visible component, so it drops to the bottom of the screen.

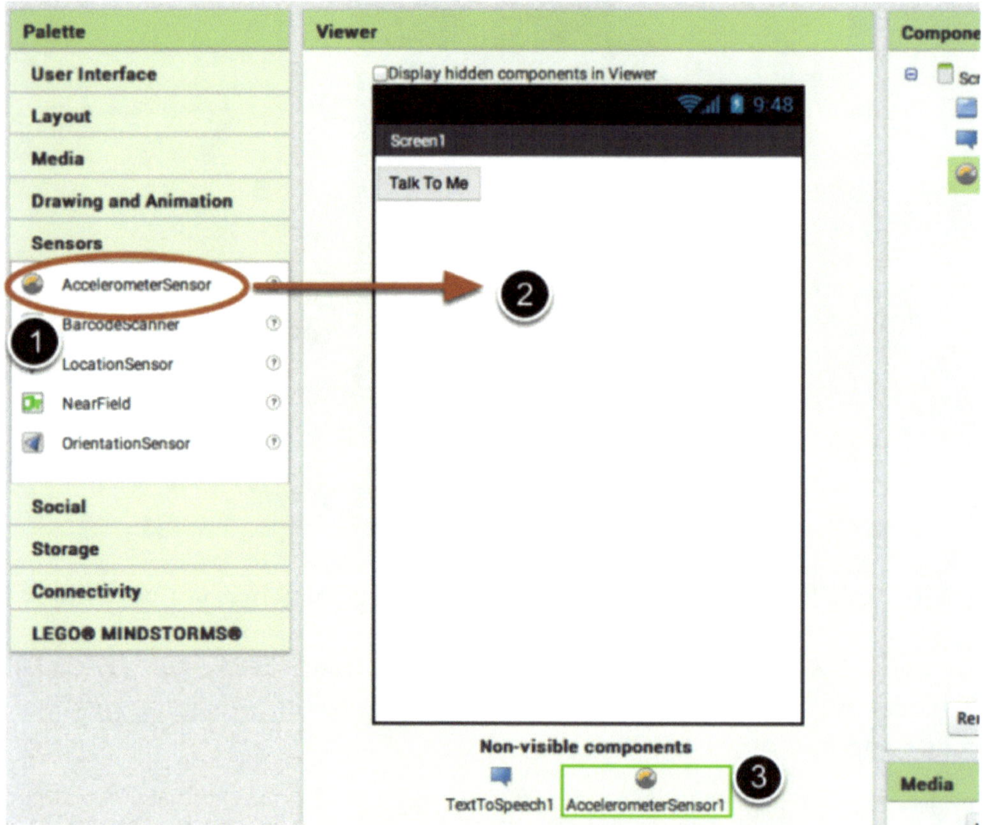

23. Go to the Blocks editor.

24. Click the AccelerometerSensor1 drawer to see its blocks and program the event. Drag out the `when AccelerometerSensor1.Shaking` block and drop it on the workspace.

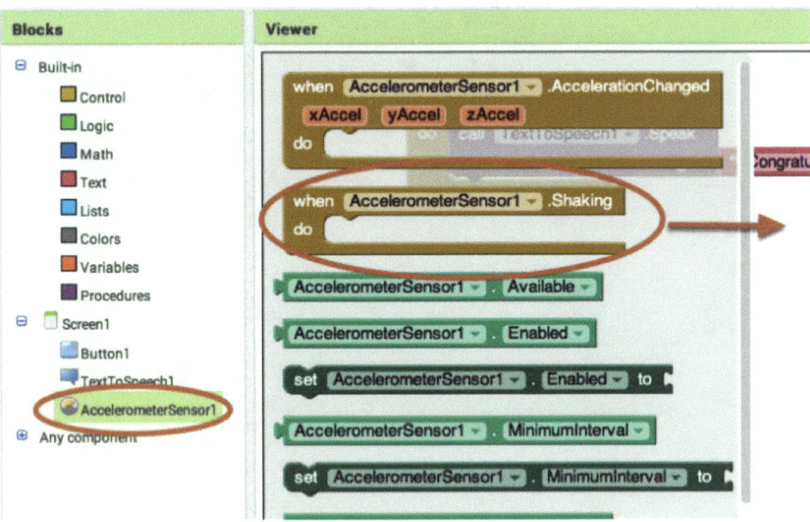

25. Copy and paste the blocks that are currently inside the `when Button1.Click` event handler. You can select the purple block, then hit the key combination on your computer to copy (CTRL + C) and then to paste (CTRL + P). You will have a second set of blocks to put inside the `when AccelerometerSensor1.Shaking` block.

Alternatively, you can drag out a new call `TextToSpeech.Speak` block from the `TextToSpeech` drawer, and a new pink `text` block from the `Text` drawer.

26. Change the phrase that is spoken when the phone is shaking. Type in "Stop shaking me!" or something funny for when the phone responds to shaking

27. Test it out! You can now shake your phone and it should respond by saying, "Stop shaking me!" or whatever phrase you put in.

Is your phone talking to you? Cool!

28. **Say Anything!** *If you are using the emulator to test your app, you may continue to this step.* Now go back to the Designer. Let's program the button click so that it causes the phone to speak whatever phrase the user put into the text box.

29. From the User Interface drawer, drag out a TextBox and put it above the Button that is already on your app screen.

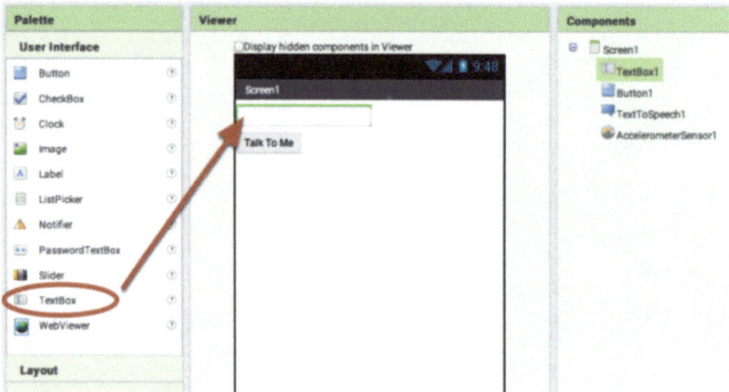

30. Go back to the `Blocks` editor.

31. On the Blocks pane, click the `TextBox1` component. Drag out the `TextBox1.Text` getter from the drawer into the Viewer. This will allow your app to speak out loud whatever is typed into the textbox (whatever is currently in the `TextBox1.Text` property).

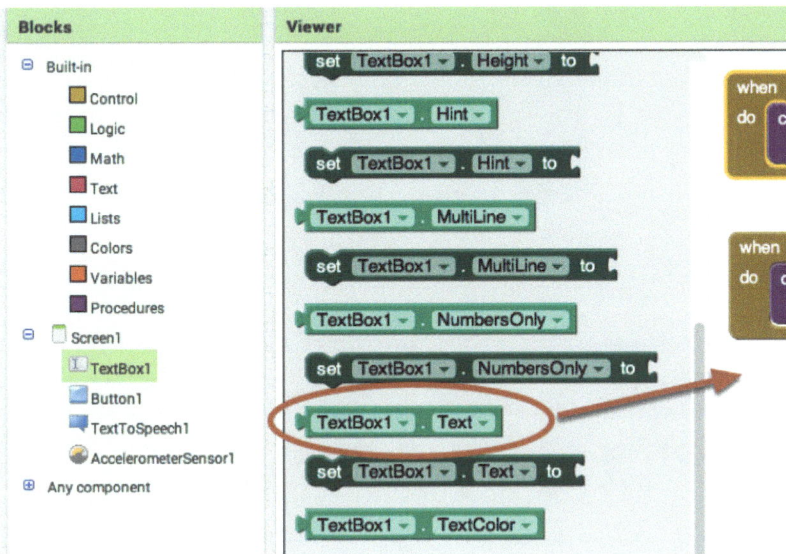

The green blocks in the `TextBox1` drawer are the getters and setters for the `TextBox1` component.

32. Pull out the "Congratulations..." text block out of `call TextToSpeech1.Speak`, and instead plug in `TextBox1.Text` onto the call block's `message` to replace it. You can throw away the pink textbox by dragging it to the `Trash` in the lower right of the workspace.

33. Test your app! Now your app has two behaviours. When the button is clicked it will speak out loud whatever words you type in the text box on the screen, or say nothing if the textbox is empty. When the phone is shaken, the app will say, "Stop shaking me!"

Explore Talk To Me further

Let's recap what you have done so far by answering the questions below:

1. Can you identify the components you use to build this app?
2. What are the built-in blocks that you used in this app
3. How do you change the colour of your button if the button is clicked?
4. What can you do to clear the text inside the textbox without deleting the text using your smartphone keyboard or cutting the text out?

Here are some ideas for extending this app. Give some thought to what else this app could do.

- Random phrase generator.
- Mad Libs: player chooses noun, verb, adjective, adverb, and person; app picks one from a list that your program.
- Name picker: useful for teachers to call on a student.

Check out the Magic 8 Ball app, an extended tutorial for Talk To Me which you can find in the official App Inventor learning resources website. Just select the Help menu in your App Inventor screen and choose Tutorials to search for it.

⬤ Project 2: Ball Bounce

In this tutorial, you will learn about animation in App Inventor by making a Ball (a sprite) bounce around on the screen (on a Canvas).

1. Go to `Projects` menu and choose `Start new project` (recall the same steps that you have learnt to create a new project in the Talk To Me app instructions).

2. Call it `BallBounce`. Remember, no spaces. But underscores are OK. Then click the BallBounce project in the list of projects to open it.

3. In the `Properties` pane, make sure that the box for `Scrollable` is empty. If there is a check sign, remove the check sign. Allowing `Scrollable` means that your app can go beyond the limit of the screen and scroll down, like reading a document or a web site. For this app, we need `Scrollable` to be disabled.

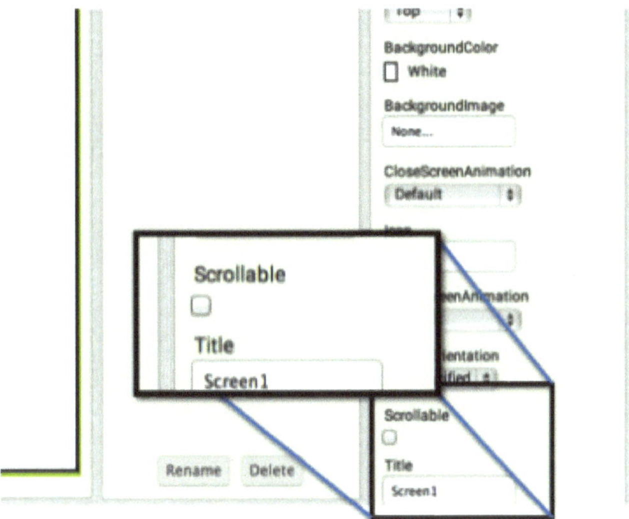

4. From the `Drawing and Animation` drawer, drag out a `Canvas` component and drop it onto the viewer.

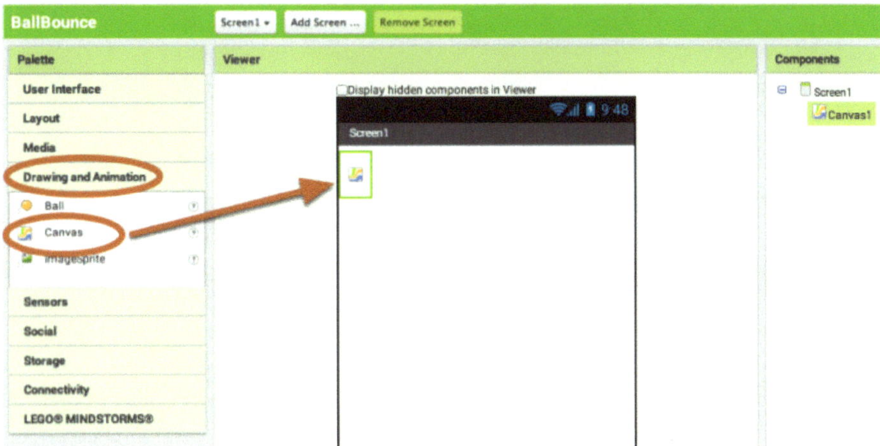

5. Change the `Height` and `Width` of the Canvas to `Fill parent`. In the `Component` window, click `Canvas1`, and look at the `Properties` windows for `Height`. Change it from `Automatic` to `Fill parent`. Do the same for `Width`, change it from `Automatic` to `Fill parent`.

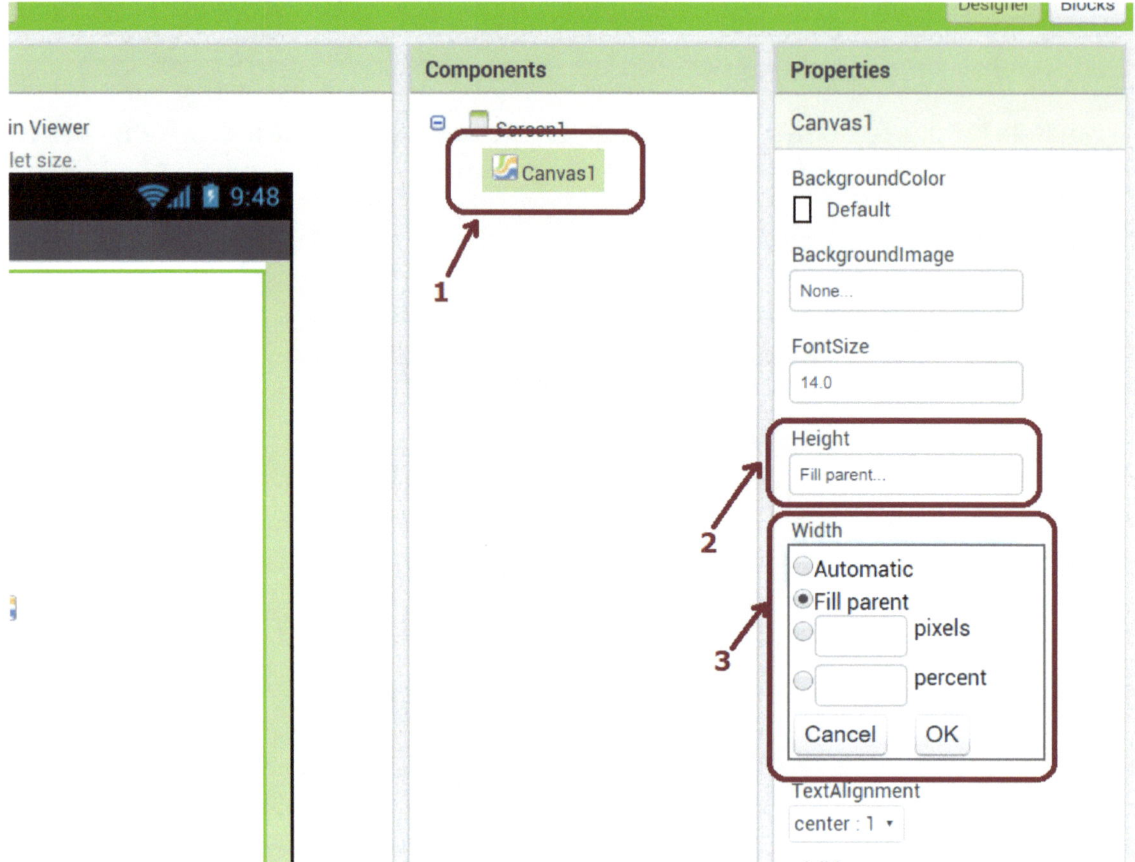

6. From the `Drawing and Animation` drawer, drag out a `Ball` component and drop it into the `Canvas` component in the viewer. You can change the size of the ball by clicking on it, and changing `Radius` in the `Properties` pane.

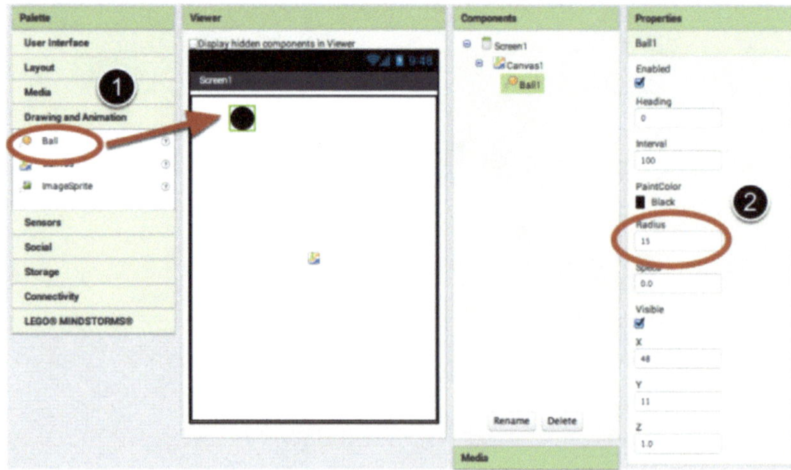

7. Open the `Blocks` editor.

8. Select `Ball1` to see its drawer, and pull out the `Ball1.Flung` event block into the Viewer. Flung refers to you making a "fling gesture" with your finger to "fling" the ball. Fling is a gesture like what a golf club does, not like how you launch Angry Birds! In App Inventor, the event handler for that type of gesture is called when Flung.

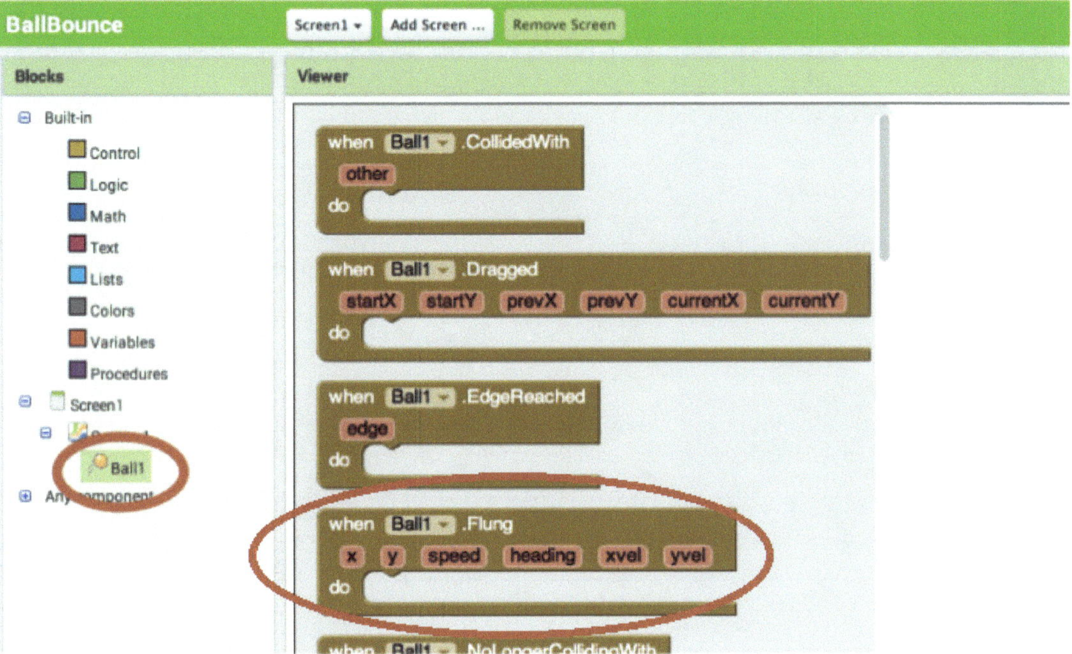

9. To set the Ball's Heading and Speed, open the Ball drawer and scroll down in the list of blocks to get the `set Ball1.Heading` and `set.Ball1.Speed`. Drag these two blocks into the viewer.

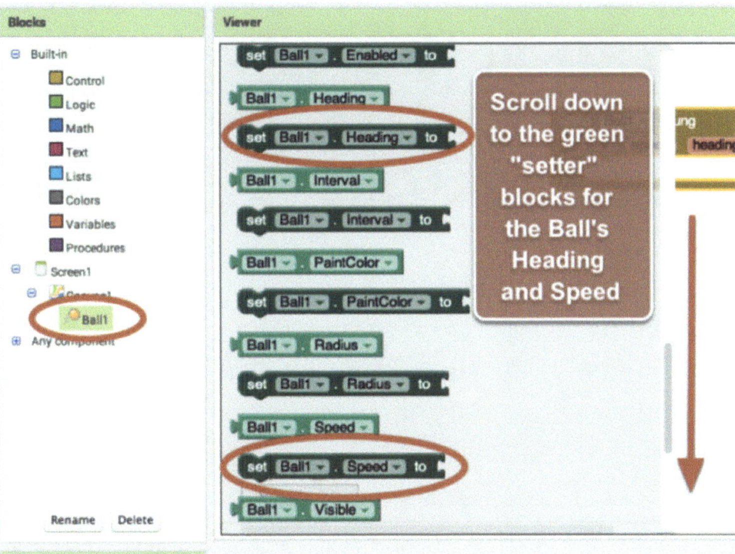

10. Plug the `set Ball1.Heading` and `set Ball1.Speed` into the Flung event handler.

11. Set the Ball's speed to be the same as the Fling gesture's speed. Mouse over the speed parameter of the Flung event, and pull out the `get  speed` block. Plug that into the `set  Ball1.Speed` block.

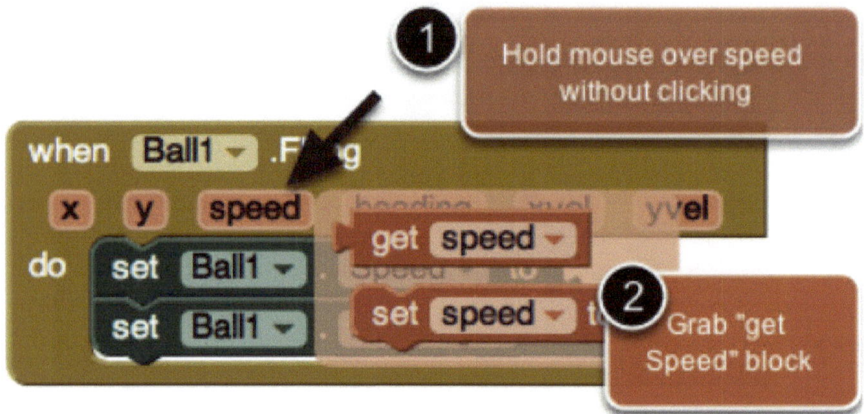

12. Do the same for the Ball's heading. Mouse over the `heading` parameter of the Flung event, and pull out the `get  heading` block. Plug that into the `set  Ball1.Heading` block. This sets the Ball's heading to be the same as the Fling gesture's heading.

13. Let's test our app. A good habit while building apps is to test while you build. App Inventor lets you do this easily because you can have a live connection between your phone (or emulator) and the App Inventor development environment. If you don't have a phone (or emulator) connected, go to the connection instructions in Section 1 and then come back to this tutorial.

Do you notice that your Ball get stuck on the side of the screen after you fling your ball? This is because the ball's heading has not changed even though it has hit the of the canvas. To make the ball "bounce" off the edge of the screen, we can add a new event handler in the programme called when EdgeReached.

14. Go into the Ball1 drawer and pull out a when Ball1.EdgeReached event block.

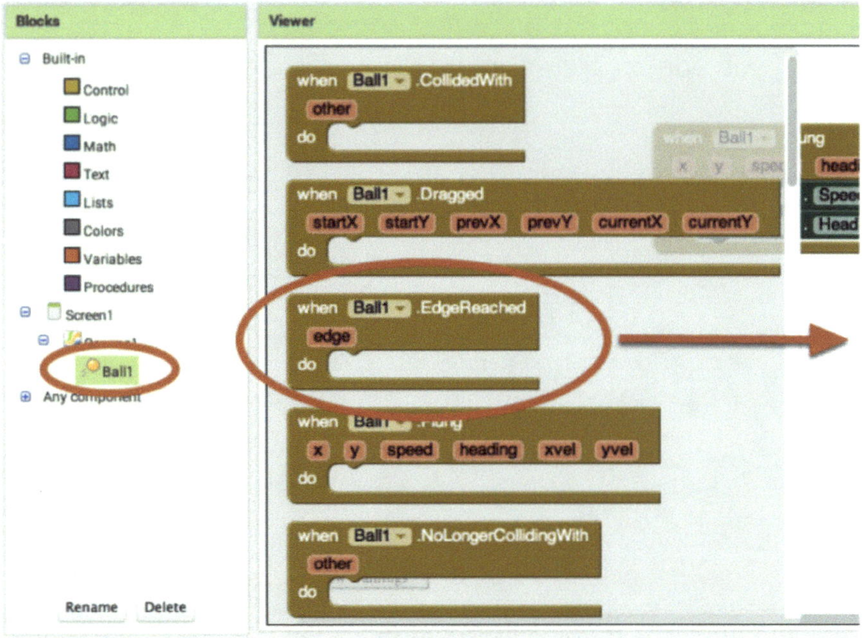

15. Go back into the `Ball1` drawer and pull out a `Ball1.Bounce` block.

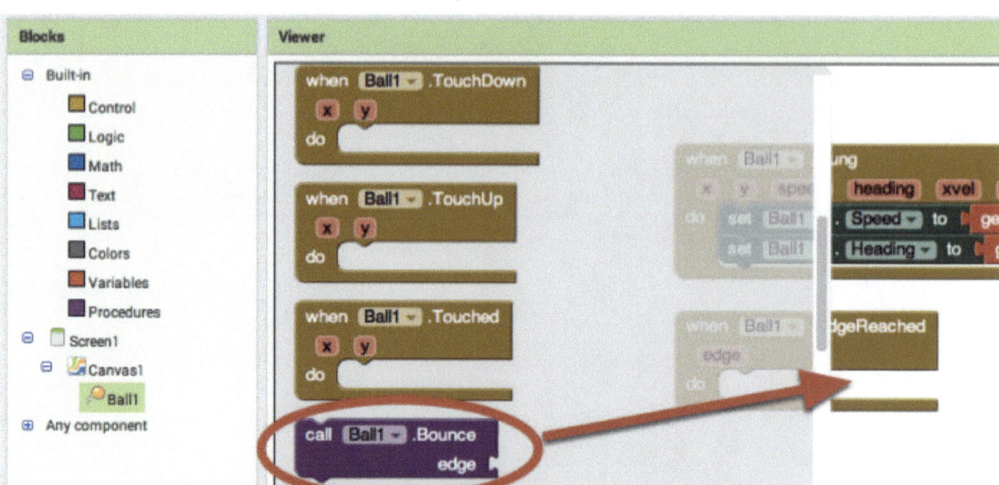

16. To add the Edge value for the `Ball.Bounce` block, mouse over the edge parameter of the `EdgeReached` event handler, and plug that into the `Ball1.Bounce` method.

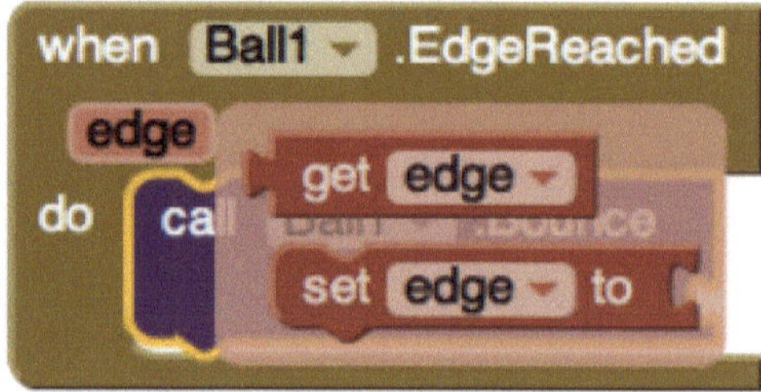

The `Ball.Bounce` method needs an edge argument, and that the `Ball1.EdgeReached` event has an "edge" as a parameter. You may get an error message until you add an argument into the method, so don't worry about it for now.

17. Your final blocks should like this.

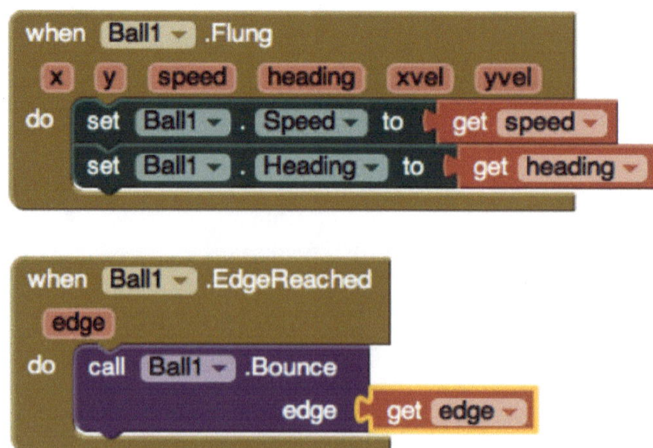

18. You're done, so test it out! Now, when you fling the ball, it should bounce off the
    edges of the canvas. Great job!

Explore Ball Bounce further

Let's recap what you have done so far by answering the questions below:

1. Can you identify the components you use to build this app?
2. How do you increase the speed of your ball when flung?
3. What would you do to programmatically stop the ball?

Here are some ideas for extending this app. The possibilities are endless!

- Change the color of the ball based on how fast it is moving or which edge it reaches.
- Scale the speed of the ball so that it slows down and stops after it gets flung.
- Give the ball obstacles or targets to hit.
- Introduce a paddle for intercepting the ball, like a Pong game.

Check out the Mini Golf app, an extended tutorial for Ball Bounce which you can find in the
official App Inventor learning resources website. Just select the `Help` menu in your App
Inventor screen and choose Tutorials to search for it.

● Project 3: Digital Doodle

This project will show you how to draw a line on the screen as you drag a finger around the phone screen.

1. Start a new project, and call it `DigitalDoodle`.

2. Set `Screen1` so that it is not `Scrollable` (remove the check sign in the box). Allowing `Scrollable` means that your app can go beyond the limit of the screen and scroll down, like reading a document or a web site. For this app, we need `Scrollable` to be disabled.

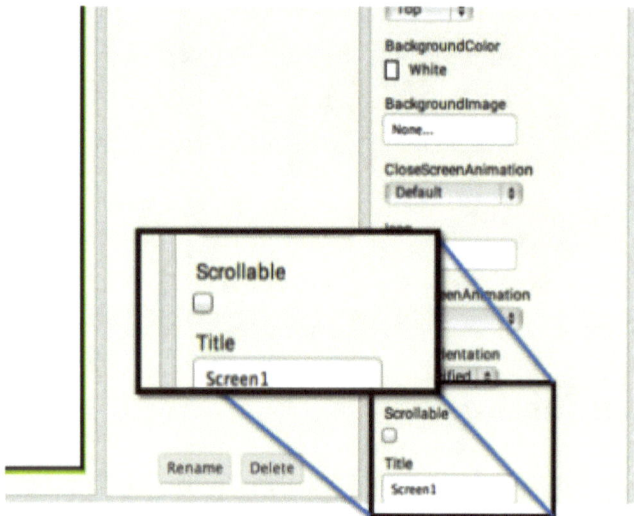

3. Add a Canvas by dragging `Canvas` from the `Drawing and Animation` drawer.

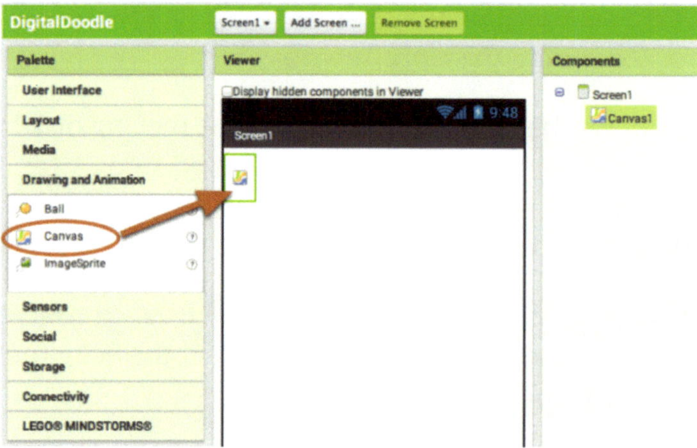

4. Change the `Height` and `Width` of the Canvas to `Fill parent`. In the `Component` window, click `Canvas1`, and look at the `Properties` windows for `Height`. Change it from `Automatic` to `Fill parent`. Do the same for `Width`, change it from `Automatic` to `Fill parent`.

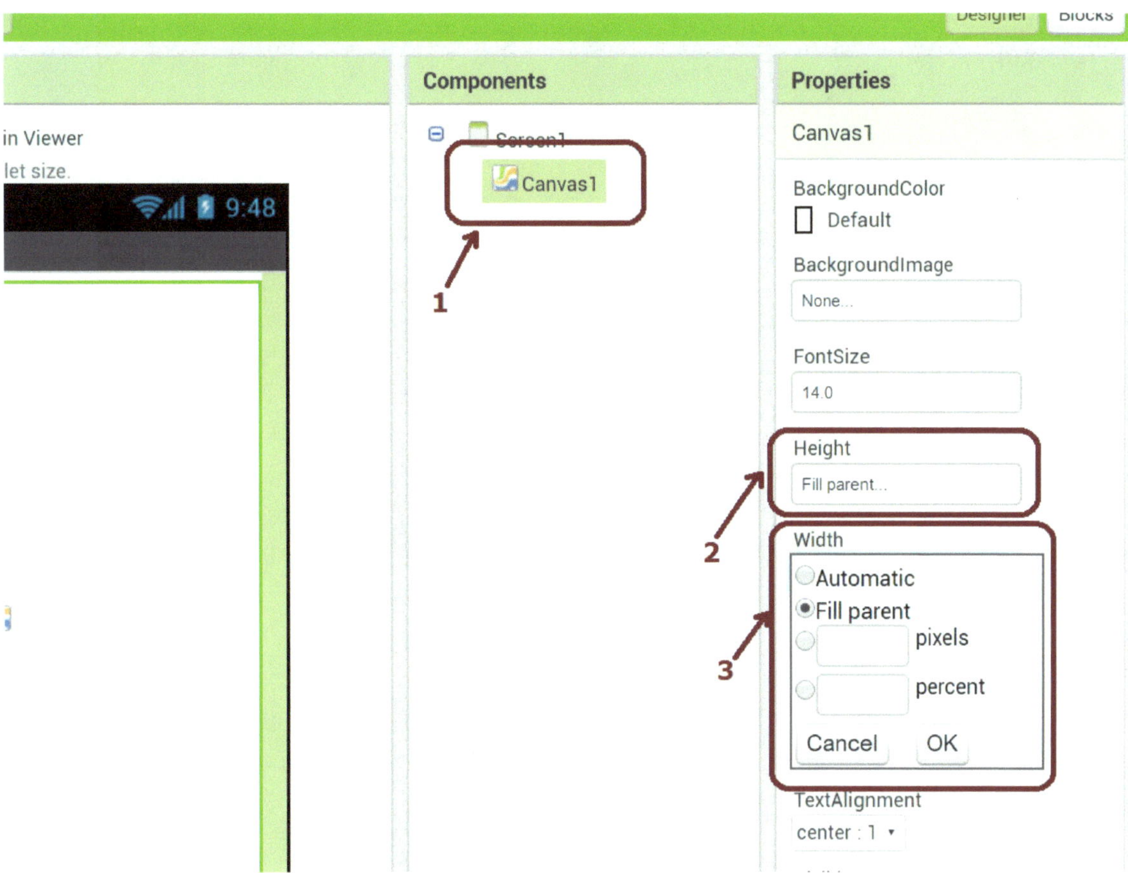

5. Switch from `Designer` to `Blocks`.

6. Select `Canvas1` to see its drawer, and pull out the `Canvas1.Dragged` event block into the Viewer.

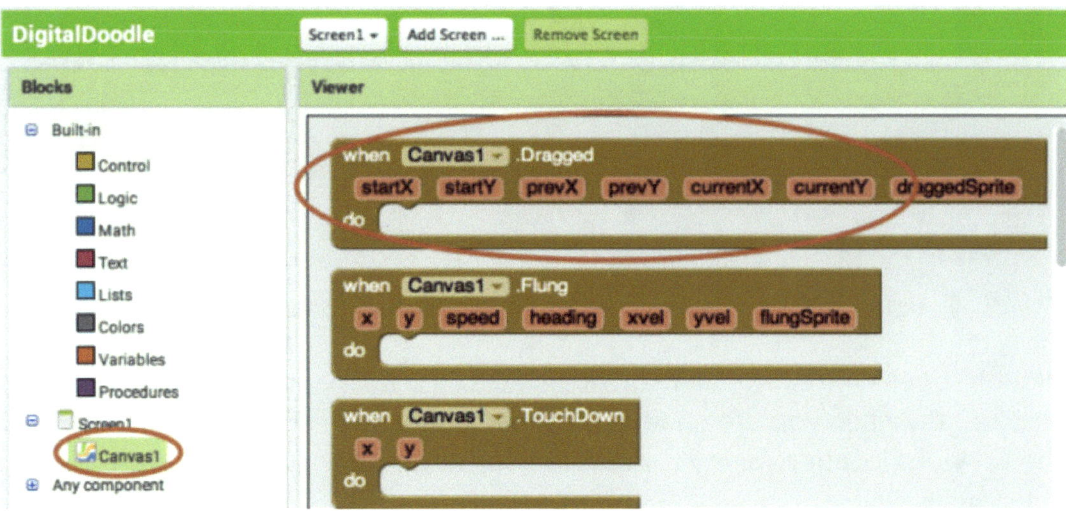

7. Select `Canvas1` to see its drawer, and pull out the `Canvas1.DrawLine` call block into the Viewer.

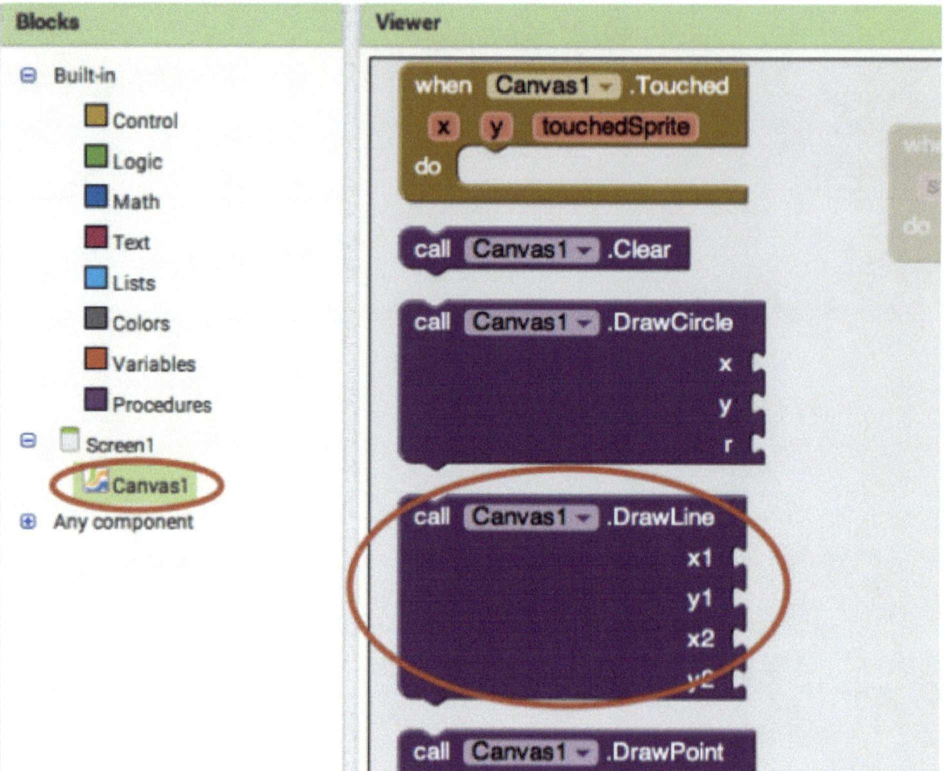

8. Mouse over prevX, prevY, currentX and currentY and pull out the their get blocks into the viewer. Fill in the x and y values in the `Canvas1` call blocks by using the get blocks.

What happens here? The `Canvas.Dragged` event will happen over and over again very rapidly while you drag a finger on the screen; it will draw a small line between the previous location (prevX, prevY) of your finger to the new location (currentX, currentY).

9. You're done, so test it out! Draw on the app. Do you see the lines?

Explore Digital Doodle further

Let's recap what you have done so far by answering the questions below:

1. Can you identify the components you use to build this app?
2. How do you change the ink colour of the lines that you draw?
3. What can you do to programmatically erase what you have drawn?

Here are some ideas for extending this app. You can probably think of many more!

- Let the user pick from a selection of ink colors.
- Change the background to a photograph or picture.
- Let the user draw dots as well as lines (hint: Use DrawCircle block).
- Add a button that turns on the camera and lets the user take a picture and then doodle on it.

Check out the PaintPot app, an extended tutorial for Digital Doodle which you can find in the official App Inventor learning resources website. Just select the `Help` menu in your App Inventor screen and choose Tutorials to search for it.

Section 4: Conceptualising Mobile App Ideas

Now comes the challenge -- coming up with your own app.

There are many ways to come up with ideas for your app. The most common way to come up with an idea for your app is by asking, "What problem do I want to solve?" Once you define your problem, your solution can serve as the objective of your app. In other words, you can build your app to solve your problem.

Ideas are part of your planning process. You also need to find out if you will be working on the app alone or in a group, how much time you have to finish it, and whether the resources you have right now, such as your computer, Internet connection, multimedia assets, and others, are enough for you to continue.

Explore More App Inventor Concepts

There are more App Inventor concepts you can explore, such as timers, sounds, movement, math, multi screens, making colors, and more. Here are some ideas and snippets and you can try out as you come up with your very own app concept.

Movement with Buttons

Move a sprite by touching a button.

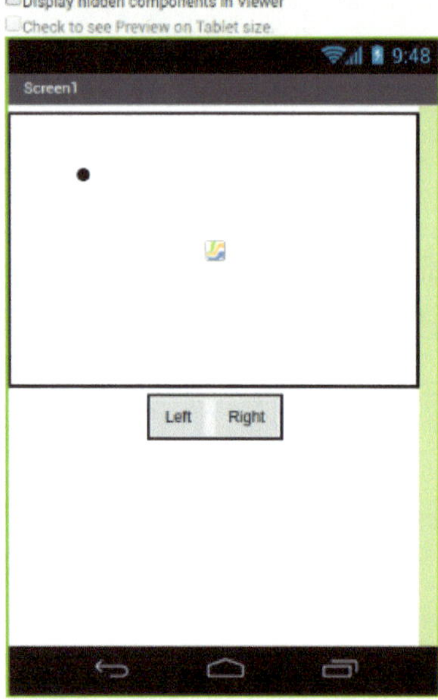

Getting Ready

You will need the following components in your design screen:
* Canvas, Sprite, Button

Blocks Editor

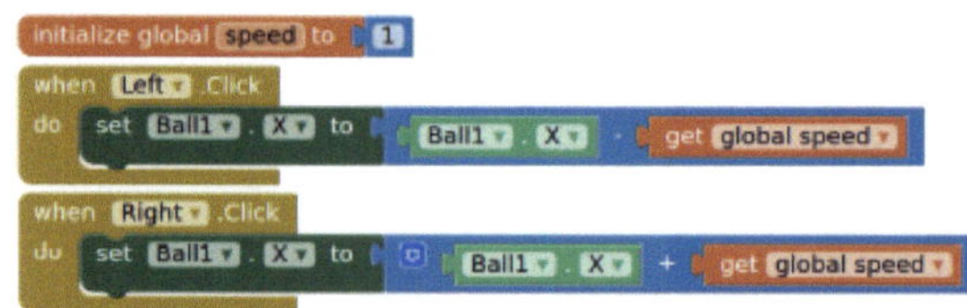

What does it mean?

Define a **speed** variable to 1 to set the how far the sprite will move each time the button is clicked.

The **Left.Click** event moves the ball to the left every time the button is touched.
The **Right.Click** event moves the ball to the right every time the button is touched.

Drag A Sprite

Move a sprite side to side by dragging
your finger

Getting Ready

You will need the following components
in your design screen:
* Canvas, ImageSprite, Clock

Blocks Editor

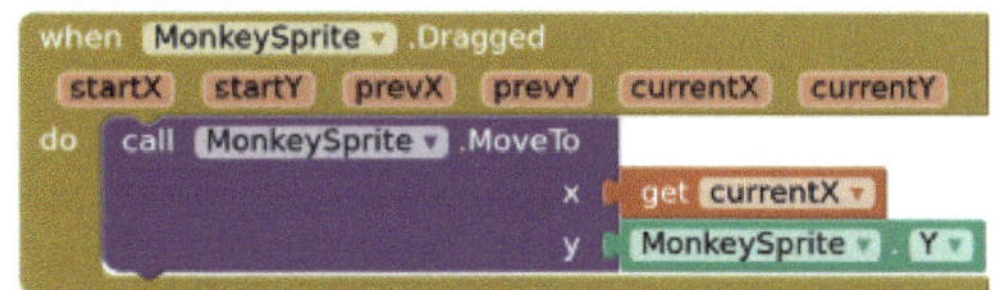

What does it mean?

While the user is dragging the sprite, **MonkeySprite.Dragged**
gets called multiple times. Each call has 6 arguments:
• **startX** and **startY**, where the user initially touched the
screen.
• **currentX** and **currentY**, where the user is currently
touching
• **prevX** and **prevY** hold whatever values were in **currentX**
and **currentY** on the previous call to the event. (On the first
call of this event, prevX and prevY are the same as startX
and startY.)
 When the user drags the MonkeySprite, it will be moved to
the new X location, **currentX**, of the drag. The Y stays the
same so the monkey can only move in
the X-direction.

Collision Detection

Make something happen when one Sprite
Collides with another.

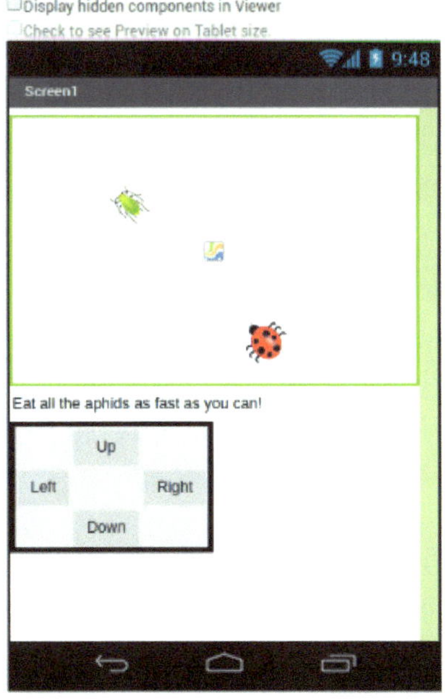

Getting Ready

You will need the following components
in your design screen:
* Canvas
* Sprite
* Button

Blocks Editor

HINT: To make your ladybug move by clicking
Buttons, check out the Movement cards.

What does it mean?

The **LadyBugCollidedWith** event is
Triggered when the Ladybug touches the
Aphid. Then this will make the Aphid
disappear.

Shaking Phone

Make something to happen when you Shake your phone.

Getting Ready

You will need the following components in your design screen:

* Image, Sound, AccelerometerSensor, Label

Blocks Editor

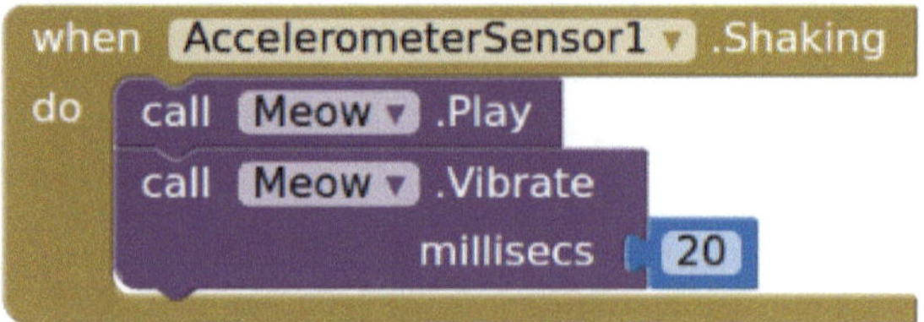

What does it mean?

The **AccelerometerSensor.Shaking** event will detect when the phone is shaking and then the Meow sound will play and the phone will vibrate for 20 milliseconds.

Creating Your Own Color

Create your own colors using the make a color block.

Getting Ready

No components are necessary to use Make color.

Blocks Editor

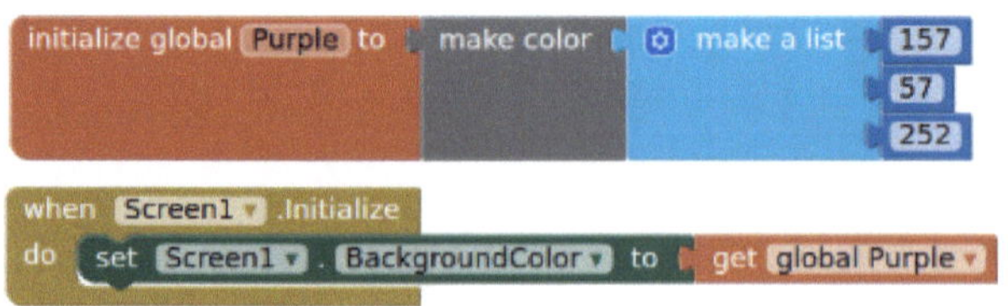

What does it mean?

Make color takes in a list of 4 numbers. The first three numbers represent the RGB values. The last is the alpha or how strong the color is. **Purple** is made from using 157 as R, 57 as G, 252 as B and 100 as alpha. **When Screen1** is initialized, the background color is set the color we created in the variable Purple.

Multiple Screens

Use multiple screens in your app.
Get the next screen by clicking a button.

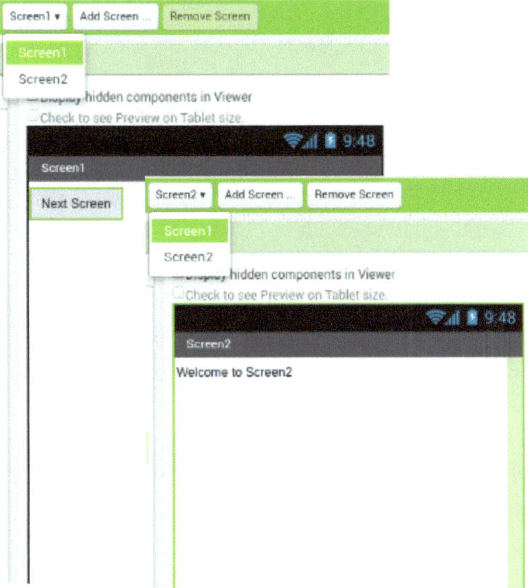

Getting Ready

You will need the following components
in your design screen:

* Screen1: Button
* Screen2: Label

Blocks Editor

(For Screen1

What does it mean?

Open another screen takes in a text block. The
text inside this block is the name of another
screen. When the button is clicked, Screen2 will
be opened.

Random Numbers

Generate random numbers to make
ImageSprites appear in random (x.y)

Getting Ready

You will need the following components
in your design screen:
* Canvas
* ImageSprite
* Clock

Blocks Editor

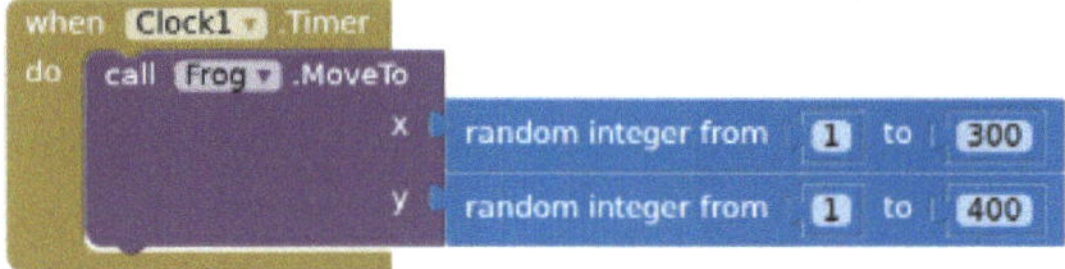

What does it mean?

When the **Clock1.Timer** event is triggered,
then **Frog.Move**To moves the frog to a
random coordinates between the values of 1
and 300 for the x coordinate and 1 and 400
for the y coordinate.

Movement with Sensors

Move an ImageSprite by tilting your phone

Getting Ready

You will need the following components in your design screen:

* Canvas, ImageSprite, OrientationSensor, Clock

Blocks Editor

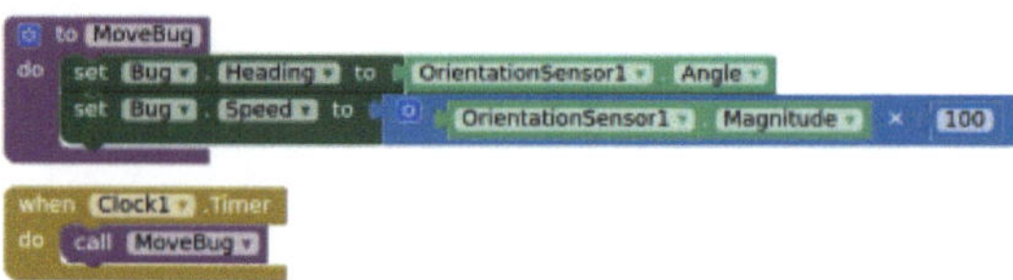

What does it mean?

A procedure called **MoveBug** was created that moves the bug in the direction that the phone is tilted.

The **OrientationSensor.Angle** is used to tell the bug which direction to move based on what angle your phone is tilted.

The **OrientationSensor.Magnitude** is used to tell the bug what speed to move based on how much tilt you are putting on your phone. Whenever the **Clock1.Timer** fires, the event **MoveBug** will be called.

Start/Stop Timed Movement

This allows the end user to touch a button to start and stop an ImageSprite moving with the passing of time.

Getting Ready

You will need the following components in your design screen:

* Canvas, ImageSprite, Clock, Button

Blocks Editor

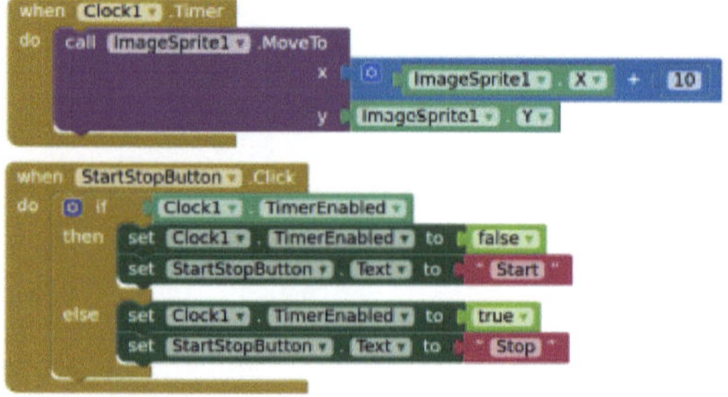

What does it mean?

When the **StartStopButton.Click** is touched, if the Clock is enabled then stop the timer and display Start on the button. This will stop the Sprite's Movement. The opposite will happen when the clock is disabled.

Drag these components on the viewer:

User Interface: Button
Media: Camera

Take a Picture

Take pictures of your friends inside of your app.

Click a button to take a picture using the Camera component. After the picture is taken, change the background of the screen to be the picture.

Click the Blocks button and snap these blocks together.

When the user clicks Button1, the user can take a picture. After the picture is taken, it becomes the background image for Screen1.

Drag these components on the viewer:

User Interface: Button   2x
Media: Camcorder   VideoPlayer
     Height: 400 px
     Width: 400 px

Make a Video

Record a video in your app.

Click a button to start recording a video using the Camcorder component. After you're finished, put the video in a Video Player component, and press a button to watch the video.

Click the Blocks button and snap these blocks together.

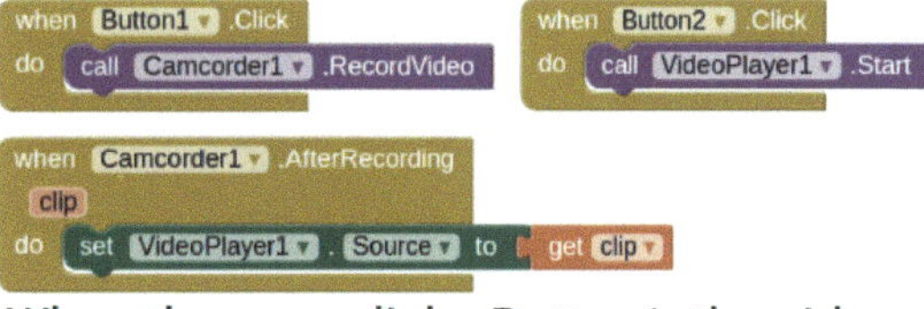

When the user clicks Button1, the video recording starts. After the recording is finished, the video is put in the video player. When the user clicks Button2, the video plays.

Look back at your projects in Section 3. Are there any apps that you can creatively change, based on the concepts shared here?

● Sketch Your App Wireframe

Once you complete your planning, the next step is to design your app. Try not to build your app right away! Steve Job once said, "Design is not just what it looks like and feels like. Design is how it works." Therefore, keep in mind about how someone who uses your app will interact with it when you design your app; in mobile app development, this is known as user experience (UX) design. Deciding the look, colour and display of your app, meanwhile, is known as user interface (UI) design.

UI and UX are often done together during your app designing process, and this section focuses on this process. For our App Inventor 2 projects, we will use wireframes. Wireframes are rough sketches of your apps using pen and paper or with a computer software.

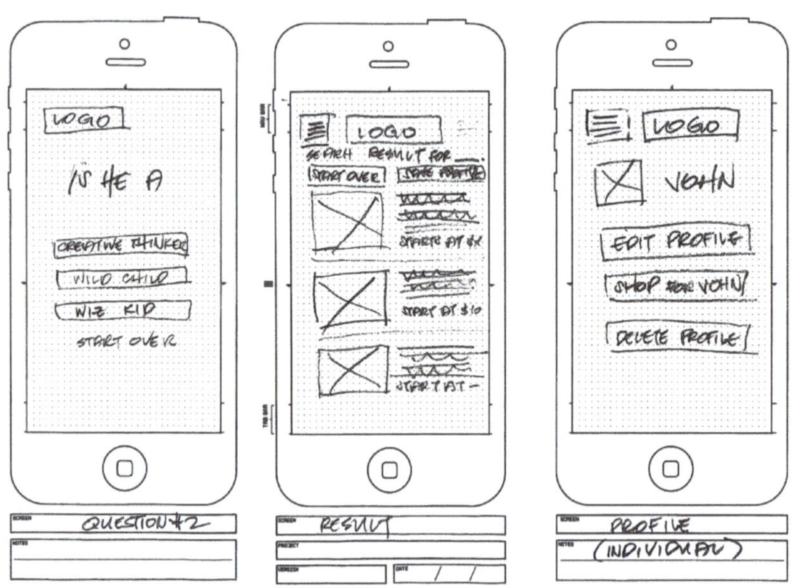

An example of a wireframe sketch for a quiz app

Wireframes are the blueprints to understand how different parts of your app works together. You can visualise your UI/UX using wireframes, and many times they also help explain the logic and flow of your app, as well as how your app works behind the scenes.

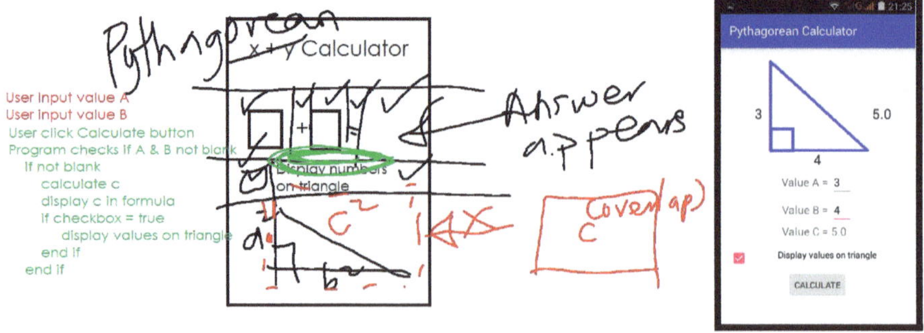

An example of a wireframe created using Microsoft Paint (left), and the finished calculator app (right)

You can use wireframes to explain to your team or anyone else about how your app works, even before you build it. This also allows you to identify problems in your design which you might not see when you first plan for your app.

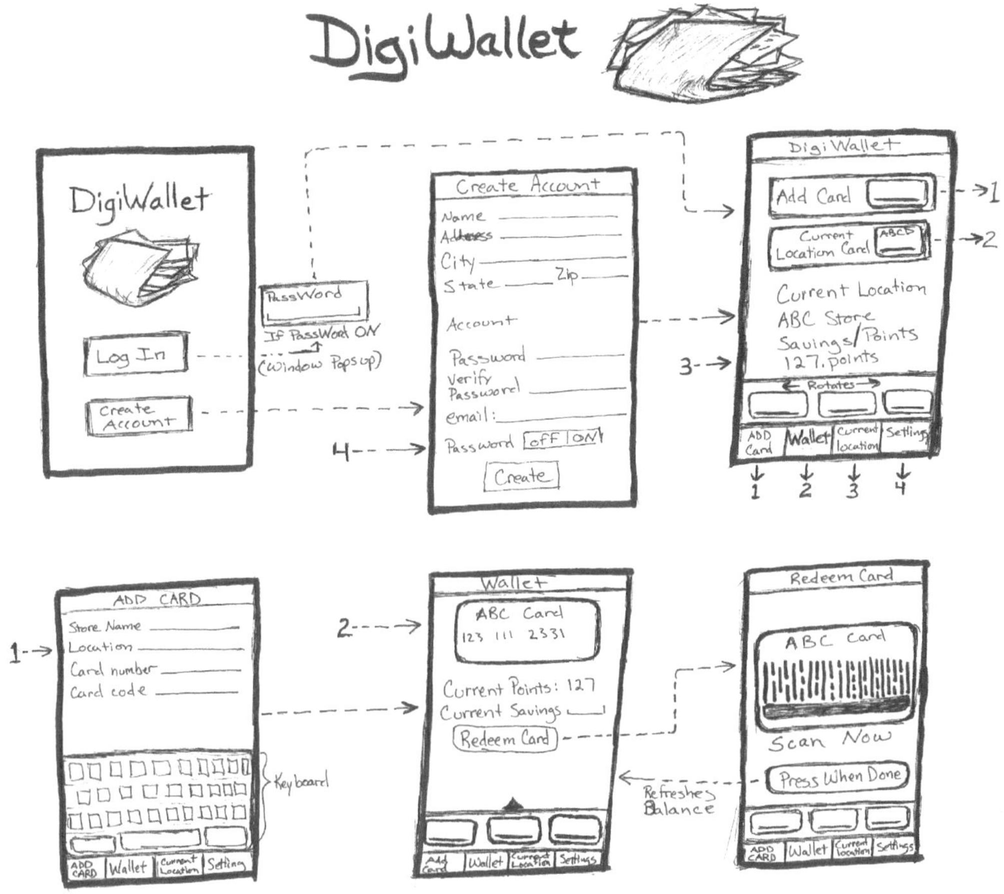

An example of a wireframe sketch for an electronic loyalty system app

Make copies of and use the following Wireframe Template provided in this book, and a pen or pencil, to conceptualise an app based on what you learnt. Mix and match the App Inventor projects you completed in Section 3 with the concepts in this section. Be creative and adventurous -- explore other functionalities within App Inventor for your new app.

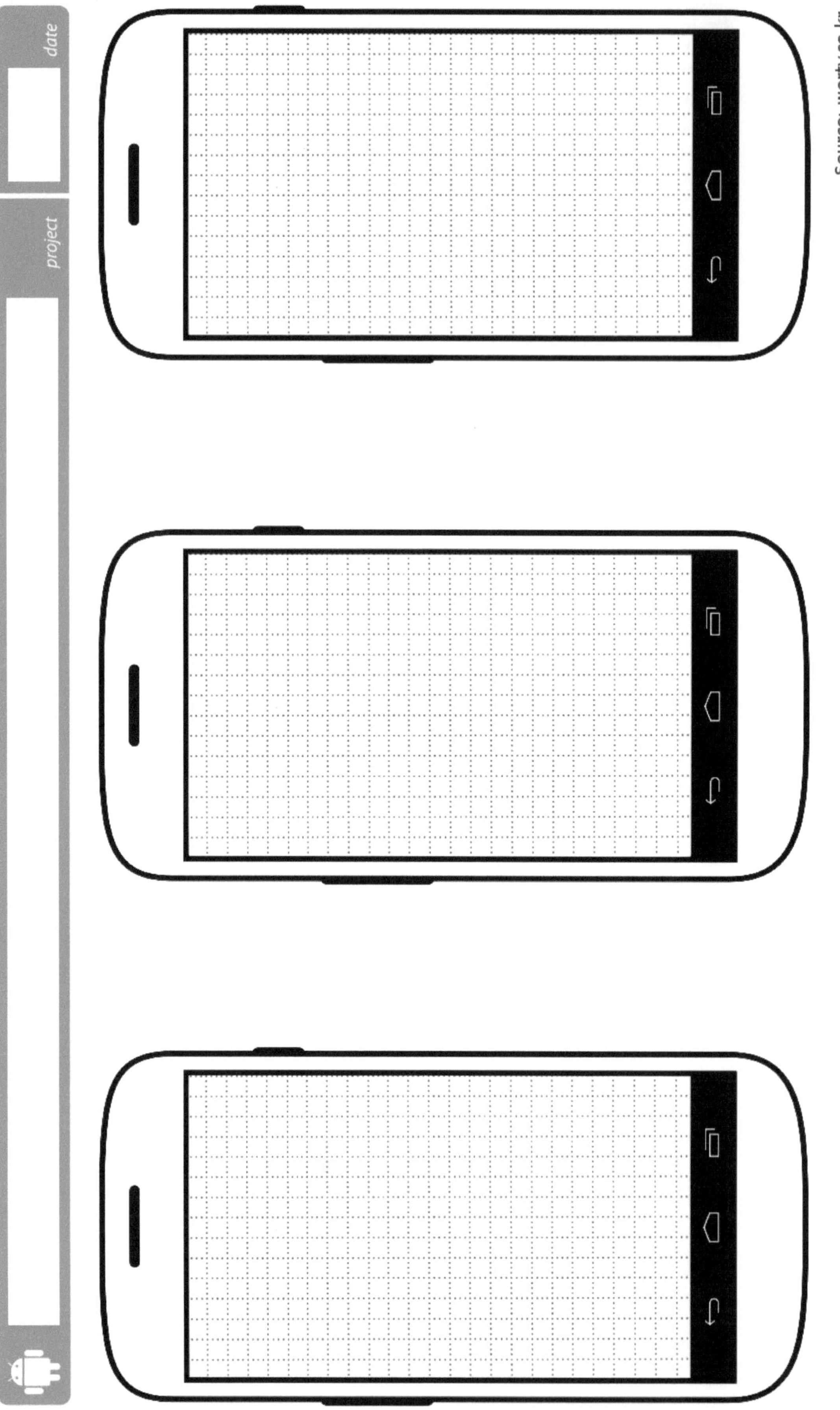

date
project
Source: werty.co.kr

Section 5: Customizing & Deploying Your Mobile App

There are many things you can do with apps built with App Inventor. On top of the concepts you explore in Section 4, you can also use `Help` and `Guide` in App Inventor's menu bar to access other advanced tutorials and learn more about App Inventor.

Here are other types of apps made using App Inventor that may require more time for you to explore:

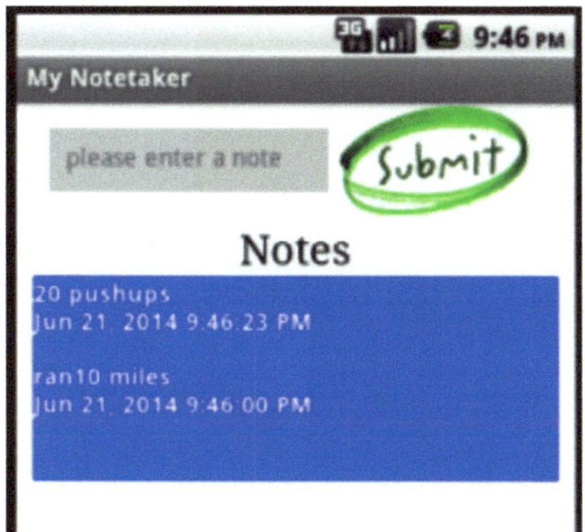

NoteTaker is an app that allows you to enter notes and see your previously entered notes. It is an example of an app with dynamic, user-generated data. The data is persistent, meaning if you close the app and reopen it, the notes will still be there. The data is not shared amongst apps or users as the notes are stored on the device, not on the web.

http://www.appinventor.org/apps2/noteTaker/NoteTaker.pdf

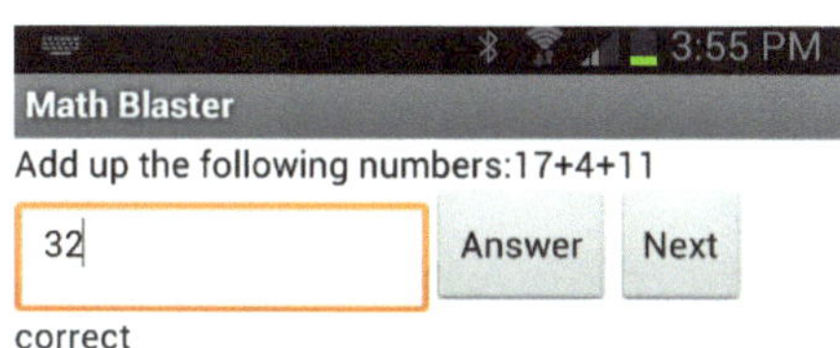

Math Blaster is a mobile app that generates arithmetic problems and checks the students answers. You can use what you learn as a template for building educational apps of all types.

http://www.appinventor.org/content/CourseInABox/userGenerated/MathBlaster

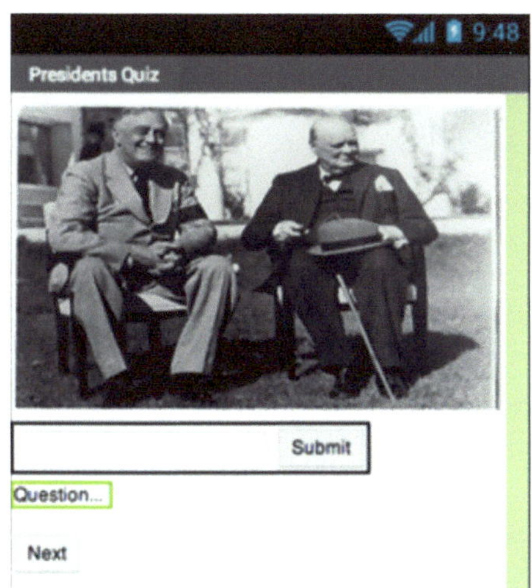

The Presidents Quiz is a trivia game about former leaders of the United States. Though this quiz is about presidents, you can use it as a template to build quizzes or study guides on any topic.

http://www.appinventor.org/bookChapters/chapter8.pdf

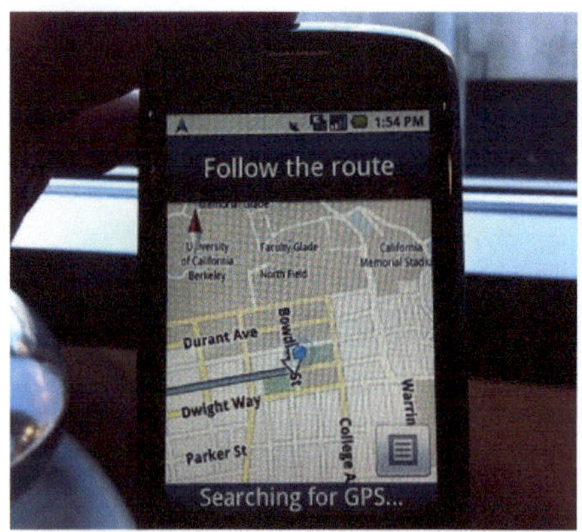

Android, Where's My Car? is an app to help you find your parked car. With this app, Android uses its location sensor to record the car's GPS coordinates and address. Later, when you reopen the app, it gives you directions from where you currently are to the remembered location.

http://www.appinventor.org/apps/android-where-s-my-car/android-where-s-my-car.pdf

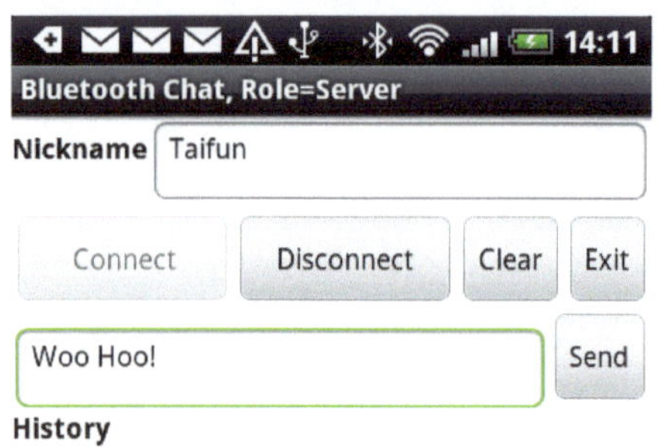

Simple Bluetooth Chat App allows you to chat with another person via a Bluetooth connection, using the Bluetooth blocks in App Inventor. Devices need to be paired at the operating system level before you can chat with each other.

http://puravidaapps.com/btchat.php

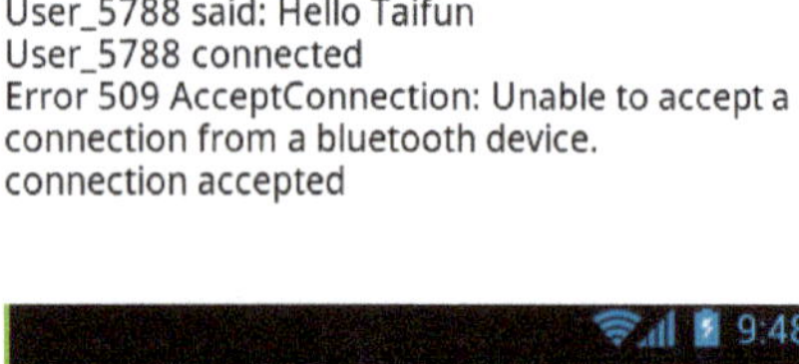

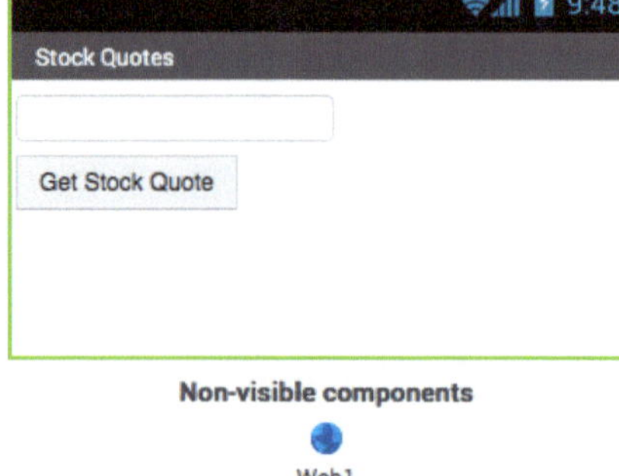

Stock Quotes enables the user to enter a stock symbol, then looks up the price of the stock on Yahoo! Finance and displays the price on the phone. This is a good tutorial if you want to learn how to use Web components and external APIs and integrate them into your app.

http://explore.appinventor.mit.edu/ai2/stockquotes

Another great place to discover App Inventor-based apps is by visiting the App Of The Month page at http://explore.appinventor.mit.edu/app-month-gallery. The webpage has different highlights based on its award categories: Most Innovative, Young Inventor, Teen Inventor, Adult Inventor, Most Creative, Best Design, and Inventor.

App of the Month   Winners!

You can find further inspiration by selecting `Gallery` in your App Inventor menu bar. You can then browse the apps and even do a remix (modification) based on the source codes of the apps, if you ever wonder how the apps are built in the first place.

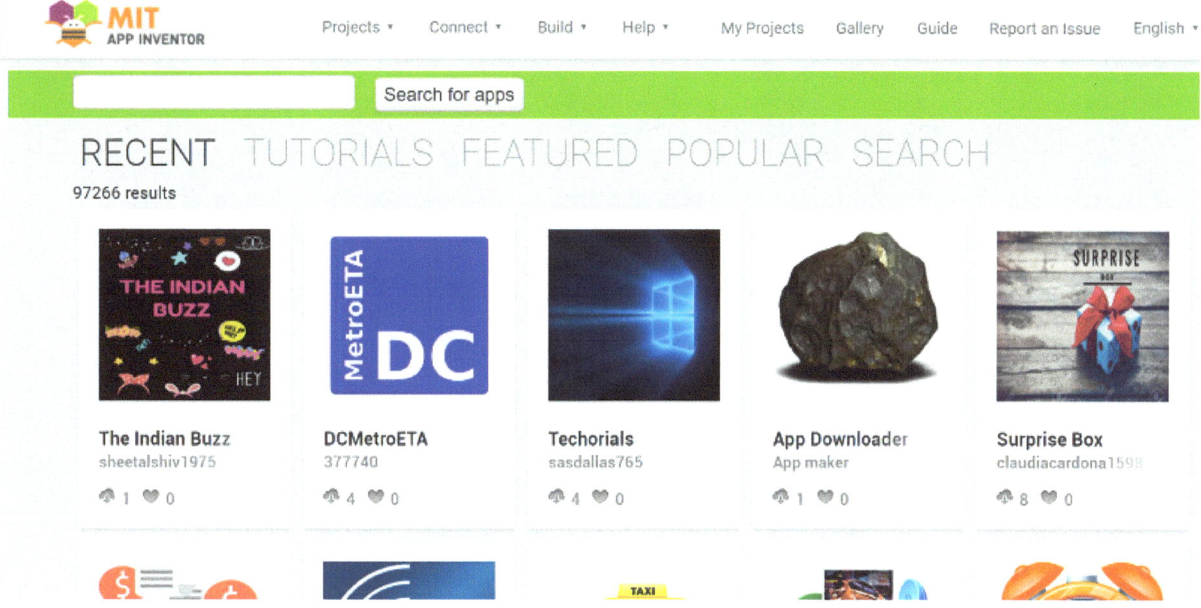

Sharing and Packaging Your App

You can share your app in an executable form (.apk) that can be installed on a device, or in source code form (.aia) that can be loaded into App Inventor and remixed. You can also distribute your app on the Google Play Store.

Sharing your app so that others can remix (.aia file)

Make sure you are viewing the list of all of your projects. If you are not, choose `Projects > My projects` in the App Inventor menu. Select the project you wish to share by checking the box next to it.

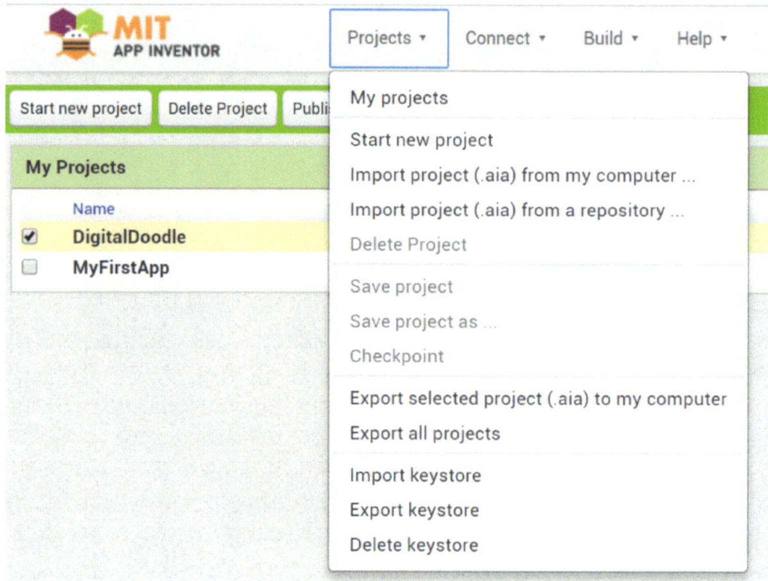

Choose `Projects > Export selected project (.aia) to my computer` to export the source code (blocks) for your project. The source code is downloaded in a `.aia` file.

If you send it to a friend, they can open it with `Projects > Import project (.aia) from my computer`.

Note: The source code (.aia) files are not executable Android programs. The source code is also not Java SDK code; it can only be loaded into App Inventor.

Sharing your app for others to install on their phone/tablet (APK file)

APK stands for Android Package Kit, and it is the package file format used by the Android operating system for distribution and installation of mobile apps. It's very much like the EXE file you use to install programs on Microsoft Windows.

Package the app (`.apk` file) by opening a project, then selecting `Build` on the App Inventor menu bar.

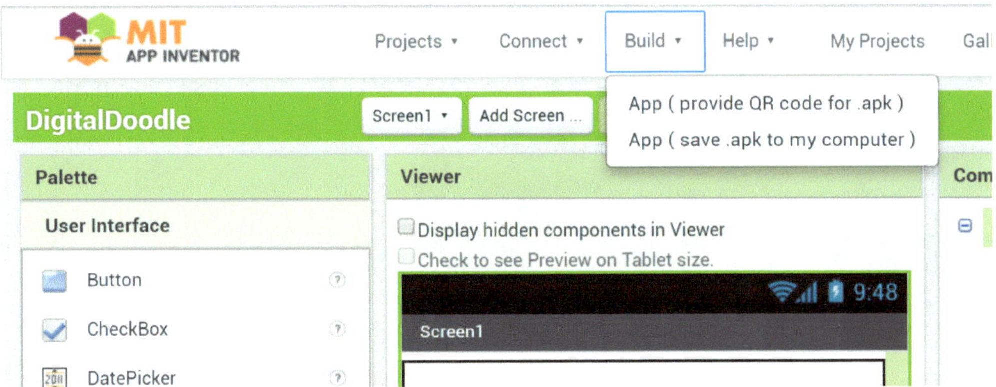

Select `App (save .apk to my computer)`. A pop-up box should alert you that your download has begun. *Note: The other option (provide QR code for .apk) produces a scannable QR code that will download the app for two hours. You can share this code with others, but they have to use it within 2 hours of your generating it.*

Once the build completes, you can email the app (".apk" file) to your friends who can install it by opening the email from their phone. If you want to distribute it more widely, you can upload it to a website that both you and your friend can access. You can also distribute your app on the Google Play Store.

NOTE: Anyone installing your app (which is an ".apk" file) will need to change the setting on their phone to allow installation of non-market applications.

> To find this setting on versions of Android prior to 4.0, go to `Settings` > `Applications` and then check the box next to **Unknown Sources**. For devices running Android 4.0 or above, go to `Settings` > `Security` or `Settings` > `Security & Screen Lock` and then check the box next to **Unknown Sources** and confirm your choice.

You're Done with the Basics! What's Next?

Now that you are familiar with MIT App Inventor, you can continue to explore and use more advanced capabilities that are normally found in mobile apps.

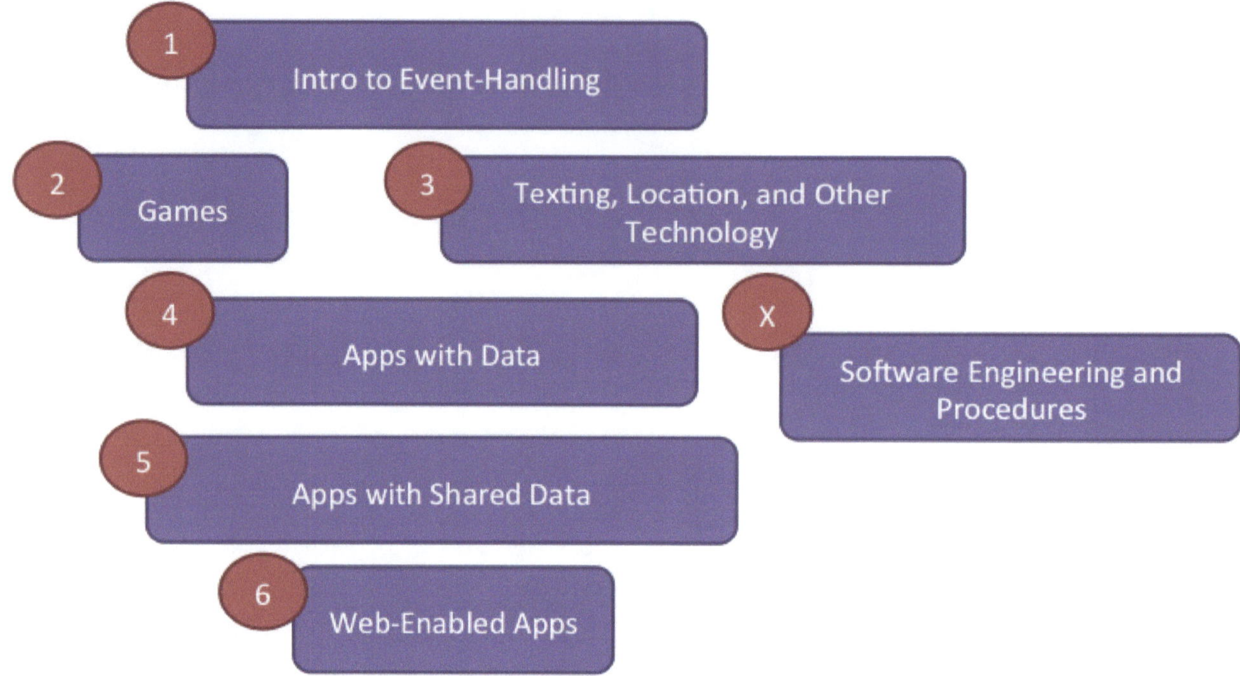

For Android app development, you should consider using the freely available Android Studio, and be ready to delve into textual programming such as Java. A great place to start learning is by visiting Udacity (www.udacity.com), an online learning platform where many of Google's official learning materials can be found. Search for the following three Udacity tutorials to get started:

1. **Android Basics: Multiscreen Apps**, where you'll learn to link multiple screens as well as playing audio and adding images to your app;
2. **Android Basics: Networking**, where you'll learn to use Web APIs, using data transfer format called JSON, and syncing data in your app; and,
3. **Android Basics: Data Storage**, where you'll learn to use databases on your app.

Meanwhile, do visit https://books.lornatimbah.com for tips and updates in order to continue your mobile app development journey.

Until then, keep learning, and have fun!

References

AppInventor.org. (n.d.). Course In A Box. Retrieved July 31, 2018, from
http://www.appinventor.org/content/CourseInABox/Intro

Computer Hope. (2017, April 26). What is an Event and Event Handler? Retrieved July 31, 2018, from https://www.computerhope.com/jargon/e/event.htm

Massachusetts Institute of Technology. (n.d.). Tutorials for App Inventor. Retrieved July 31, 2018, from http://appinventor.mit.edu/explore/ai2/tutorials.html

Hariprasad, P. (2015, August 10). Wireframes Testing - Part I. Retrieved July 30, 2018, from
http://curioustester.blogspot.com/2015/08/wireframes-testing-part-i.html

JLR Interface Design. (1970, January 01). App WireFrame. Retrieved July 30, 2018, from
http://jlrbacktoschool.blogspot.com/2012/03/app-wireframe.html

Nam Insik Portfolio site. (2013, May 20). 안드로이드 스케치 템플릿. Retrieved July 30, 2018, from http://naminsik.com/blog/2132

QUICK TIPS FOR EDUCATORS

If you are using this book for your class, then thank you! Here are a few tips to make learning app development more fun and engaging.

1 Follow the Build-Conceptualise-Customise-Create Method

Remember to focus on the Smiley Face sections. Let your learners jump right into building the apps once setup is ready.

2 Try the Questions to Expand Their Knowledge of the Topics

Each project comes with a set of questions, which builds up on the concepts. They will be useful when students need to customise and create new apps.

3 Let Your Students Lead the Class

Set a clear expectation of what they should achieve at the end of your lessons. Then, let them lead each other and be accountable for the end result. Allow free movement so that better students can help the others to catch up on the projects.

4 Challenge Different Dimensions of Knowledge

Take this chance to combine language and presentation skills, video or photo taking projects, web designing skills, curating history notes, or problem solving their existing school subjects.

Visit https://books.lornatimbah.com for more teaching tips, updates & resources on App Inventor 2.

BONUS INFO: Learning Strategies for STEM Subjects

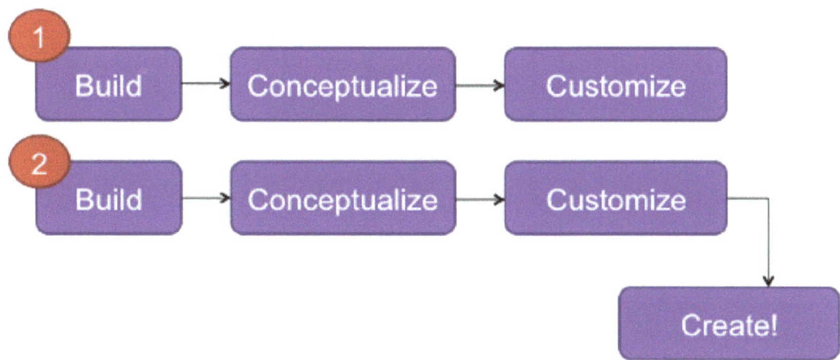

The projects provided in this book follow a do-first structure that has worked well in motivating learners to learn. This methodology is called "Build-Conceptualise-Customise-Create" and has been very successfully used in many classrooms and learning environments. This method can easily be replicated onto other STEM subjects that allow for hands-on or project-based activities.

- **Build It**: Introduce a topic but keep it brief. Within minutes, get the learners building an interesting app, using a step-by-step tutorial.
- **Conceptualise It**: After the learners complete the projects, break them into small groups to discuss conceptual questions about the app, then discuss as a class.
- **Customise It**: After the discussion session, assign customization tasks in which learners add interesting features to the app they just built.
- **Create It**: After two or three iterations of the Build-Conceptualise-Customise process, give the learners the freedom to choose an app of personal interest to them.

As an example, here is an outline of my lesson plan for short courses. Remember, focus on the topics with the Smiley Face ● to get the most out of the learning experience.

Topic	Learning Method	Duration
Introducing App Inventor and Setting Up Your App Inventor Environment	Lecture & Demonstration	30-60 minutes
Project 1: Talk to Me	Hands-on Tutorial	60 minutes
Explore Project 1	Q & A and group discussion	15 minutes
Projects 2 and 3	Hands-on Tutorial, individually in pairs	60 minutes
Explore Projects 2 and 3	Q & A and group discussion	15 minutes
Conceptualising a New App: Design	Brainstorm and exercise	15 minutes
Conceptualising a New App: Develop	Hands-on Exercise & group work	60 minutes
Conceptualising a New App: Present and Pitch	Group demonstration	3 minutes each

www.ingramcontent.com/pod-product-compliance
Lightning Source LLC
Chambersburg PA
CBHW042046110726
48006CB00002B/303